Motorbooks International

MIL-TECH SERIES

TOMAHAWK

CRUISE MISSILE

Nigel Macknight

First published 1995 by Motorbooks
International Publishers & Wholesalers, P O
Box 2, 729 Prospect Avenue, Osceola, WI
54020, USA

Library of Congress Cataloging-in-
Publication Data
Macknight, Nigel.
    Tomahawk cruise missile/Nigel
Macknight.
        p. cm.—(Motorbooks International
mil-tech series)
    Includes index.
    ISBN 0-87938-717-3
    1. Tomahawk (Guided missile)—
History. 2. Cruise missiles—History
I. Title   II. Series.
UG1312.C7M33 1995
623.4'519—dc20   94-39389

Photo credits: All of the photos
reproduced in this book were supplied by
McDonnell Douglas Aerospace-East,
except: front and back covers, see credits
at captions below; page 7, Sperry
Corporation; page 8, General Motors
Institute; page 9, US National Archives;
page 10, US National Air & Space Museum;
page 11, Royal Aerospace Establishment;
pages 12-14, USAF; page 15, Imperial War
Museum; page 16, USAF; page 19, US
National Archives; page 20, USAF; page 22,
USAF; page 23, Northrop; page 24, USAF;
pages 27-29, USAF; page 30, US Navy; page
32, US Navy; page 33, USAF; page 36,
Williams International; page 37, USAF;
pages 40-41, Vought Corporation; page 43,
Joint Cruise Missile Project Office; page 50,
Williams International; page 60, General
Dynamics; pages 64-65, General Dynamics;
page 82, Hughes Missile Systems Company;
page 91, General Dynamics

Diagram credits: All diagrams by Pete
West, except: pages 56-57, Peggy Greenlee

Page design: Macknight International

Page make-up: Flexitype, Peterborough,
England

On the front cover: A Tomahawk streaks
from the armored box launcher of a US
Navy ship. *McDonnell Douglas Aerospace-
East*

On the back cover: Spectacular sequence
showing a Tomahawk emerging from the
water. Moments later, its wings, tail fins
and engine air intake will have deployed,
allowing the missile to cruise towards its
target. Doors in the missile's flanks open to
let the wings swing out, then close again to
streamline the slots through which the
wings protrude. *General Dynamics*

Printed and bound in the United States of
America

Contents

Acknowledgments

This book was made possible by the input of several individuals and organizations whose generous assistance is gratefully acknowledged. They include: Dave Arnold, Jack Bierk, Lloyd Carpenter, Mike Coggins, Jack Corcoran, Bob Harmon, Barbara Huddleston, and Bruce Reid at McDonnell Douglas Aerospace-East; Susan Boyd, Bob Holsapple and Matt Worthington at the US Navy's Program Executive Office for Cruise Missiles and UAVs; Bob Gregory at Hughes Missile Systems Division; and Christina Pearce at Williams International.

Dr. Kenneth Werrell, Professor of History at Radford University, Virginia, deserves special thanks. His book, *The Evolution of the Cruise Missile*, proved invaluable when I came to research the origins of the Tomahawk.

Finally, my thanks to Michael Dregni, Greg Field, Jane Mausser, and Tim Parker at Motorbooks International.

Nigel Macknight, April 1994

Introduction

The Cruise Missile Concept

Striking targets from afar is a longstanding military objective. In this respect, the cruise missiles of today extend a capability that began with the invention of the catapult. As technology progressed, the means of dealing a "stand-off" blow became ever more complex. The rifle was a big step forward, the cruise missile another. The Tomahawk has represented the pinnacle of cruise missile technology for a time, but it will inevitably be eclipsed.

Cruise missiles offer the ability to destroy heavily-defended targets without risking aircrews. Being small, cruise missiles present a difficult target for enemy defenses to locate and destroy in flight, particularly when they hug the contours of the earth, hiding in the "clutter": the unwanted echoes of ground features that confuse the observation of signals on a radar screen. On the ground, their small size makes them easy to conceal, should that be necessary. The absence of a human pilot gives the cruise missile several advantages. Higher G-forces can be sustained when maneuvering, and freedom from the natural instinct for self-preservation makes the cruise missile a truly fearless foe.

Although cruise missiles carry a smaller fuel load than most manned aircraft, the available fuel goes a long way, as it can all be expended on the out flight—there being no need to retain any for a return journey!

Cruise missiles possess a rich conceptual and technological heritage. The Tomahawk itself has had an exceptionally diverse history, versions having been developed for air-launching, ground-launching and sea-launching. Today, only sea-launched Tomahawks are fielded: there is a small family of them, each optimized for a specific role. Deployed on surface vessels and submarines that can traverse the globe, they provide the US Navy with an unparalleled stand-off strike capability against ships and fixed targets ashore, complementing carrier-based aircraft.

Tomahawks are versatile. They can be launched horizontally or vertically with equal effectiveness, and they can fly in all weather conditions, by day or by night.

The Tomahawk gained international prominence as a symbol of America's high-technology edge during Operation Desert Storm, the forty-two-day military action which followed Iraq's invasion of Kuwait—when nearly 300 were launched against heavily-defended strategic targets, achieving a hit rate in excess of 90 percent. The missile's deep-strike capability was employed to maximum effect, severely disrupting Iraq's ability to wage war. Many of the Tomahawks were launched in the opening stages of the conflict, to knock out key Iraqi communications links and air defenses prior to strikes by manned aircraft.

This book summarizes the development of the cruise missile, examines the Tomahawk in some depth, then casts a glance at future prospects.

The Tomahawk gained international prominence as a symbol of America's high-technology edge during Operation Desert Storm, the forty-two-day military action which followed Iraq's invasion of Kuwait—when nearly 300 were launched against heavily-defended strategic targets, achieving a hit rate in excess of 90 percent.

Chapter 1

Cruise Missile Evolution

The Tomahawk's Ancestors

In one form or another, the cruise missile concept has been around for a long time. Even prior to World War I—when powered flight was in its first decade—forward-thinking individuals in several countries were advocating the idea of an unmanned, automatically-piloted airplane to deliver an explosive punch from afar. They referred to it as the "flying bomb," or, drawing a somewhat surreal air-as-water analogy, the "aerial torpedo." Its significance was likened in magnitude to the invention of gunpowder by the more enthusiastic advocates. In 1915, a newspaper article lauded the weapon as, "A device likely to revolutionize modern warfare."

If the cruise missile does, indeed, prove to be "the gun of the future," as one early supporter suggested, historians will probably cite the Gulf War of 1991 as the watershed: the point in time when even the most hardened of cynics had to acknowledge its value. Tomahawks launched from ships in the comparative safety of the Red Sea and the Persian Gulf, flew hundreds of miles to their destinations deep within Iraqi territory, eluding enemy defenses to strike their targets with pinpoint accuracy.

This was a far cry from the first faltering experiments with "flying bombs." These owed their limited success to the gyroscope: a device containing a disc rotating on an axis that can turn freely in any direction, so that the disc maintains the same orientation irrespective of the movement of its surroundings— an ideal basis for a navigation system.

The experiments resulted from a collaboration between Elmer A. Sperry, the founder of Sperry Gyroscope Company, and Peter C. Hewitt, the inventor of the mercury vapor lamp. Their efforts produced a most convincing demonstration of the potential capabilities of the "aerial torpedo" on 12 September 1916, when a gyroscope-guided seaplane automatically climbed to a predetermined altitude, held a satisfactory compass course, flew a set distance, dove, and would have impacted the predesignated spot but for the intervention of a human "monitor" pilot placed aboard as a precautionary measure— Lawrence Sperry, Elmer Sperry's son.

This demonstration was conducted under the watchful eye of an invited US Navy observer. The US Army had been approached first, but had not bothered to reply!

Based on the 12 September demonstration, Lawrence Sperry was quoted as saying that an accuracy of 3 miles (4.8km) could be achieved at a range of 10 miles (16km), and an accuracy of 8 miles (12.8km) could be achieved at a range of 100 miles (160km). The US Navy observer, Lieutenant T.W. Wilkinson, Jr., appraising the benefits and drawbacks of the device, noted that it had a longer range than any gun, although it was expensive, and required complex launching facilities. Wilkinson opined that, "The moral effect of such devices may be great. They are practically indestructible, unless a well-aimed shot disables the engine or control devices, and they cannot be driven off."

However, Wilkinson considered that its "use in long-range attacks against forts and cities is of doubtful military value on account of the difficulty of striking at any desired point, rather than at random within the limits of the city or fortress."

Spurred by the entry of the United States into World War I in 1917, the US Navy/Sperry experiments intensified. With US Navy funding, five Curtiss N-9 seaplanes fitted with Sperry control sets made over 100 test flights from Amityville, Long Island. Human pilots aboard the aircraft undertook the take-offs and landings, and monitored the performance of the automatic system. A diminutive new, unmanned device (faster than the N-9) followed. It was launched from a dolly on a short length of rail track, aided by a catapult system, and this procedure proved desperately accident-prone. Once a monitor pilot was placed aboard, prospects improved. However, Lawrence Sperry was fortunate to escape uninjured when the missile, temporarily fitted with skis, crashed on take-off and was wrecked.

During this time, efforts to develop "flying bombs" were also under way in Europe—in Great Britain, in particular. Professor A.M. Low demonstrated a radio-controlled "flying bomb" to British

Elmer A. Sperry, the founder of Sperry Gyroscope Company, whose collaborative effort with Peter C. Hewitt, the inventor of the mercury vapor lamp, demonstrated the potential capabilities of the gyroscope-guided "aerial torpedo."

War Office officials on 21 March 1917, with the intention of intercepting zeppelins and attacking ground targets. H.P. Folland designed a similar missile built by the Royal Aircraft Factory. Both were small, lightweight craft powered by the same type of 35hp engine, and both failed dismally.

When World War I ended, the US Navy/Sperry experiments continued apace, despite numerous setbacks. Even after Elmer Sperry bowed out of the project, the tests went on. A variety of configurations had been tested by the time the Navy canceled the project in 1922. Accuracy had improved considerably, but incessant reliability problems had hampered progress.

By now, the US Army had an interest in the concept. The turning point had been a demonstration flight staged in late 1917, when a Curtiss N-9 flew over 7 miles (11.2km) automatically. A few days later, Major General George O. Squier, who had been present at the demonstration, wrote the Chairman of the Aircraft Board that the "flying bomb" should be developed with all haste. The upshot of Squier's recommendation was the formation of a four-man investigative board to assess the device's potential, and the awarding of a contract to develop it. The recipient of the contract was a member of the investigative board (the only member to champion the weapon), Charles F. Kettering: the inventor of the automobile self-starter, and later to become vice-president of General Motors. Kettering formed a team at Dayton, Ohio, which included Orville Wright—for Dayton Wright Airplane would develop the airframe—and gyroscope

Spurred by the entry of the United States into World War I in 1917, the US Navy/Sperry experimental program sired this diminutive device. It was launched from a dolly on a short length of rail track, aided by a catapult system—a procedure that proved desperately accident-prone.

wizard Elmer Sperry. Kettering's Dayton Metal Products company would supply the control system.

This hugely talented team created the Liberty Eagle—more popularly known as the Kettering Bug—a biplane even smaller than the US Navy/Sperry device, with a pronounced wing dihedral. Simplicity was the keynote: it had no ailerons, and was covered with muslin and brown wrapping paper doped with glycerine and creosote. For automatic flights, an air impeller actuated a standard National Cash Register counter which "measured" the distance flown. After a predetermined number of turns, this cut the ignition and folded the wings. Monitor pilots flew aboard the Bug for the initial test flights. After that, the missile took off from a dolly on a rail track, but without the aid of a catapult. Some of the early flights lasted mere seconds, but on 4 October 1918, a Bug flew for 45 minutes in wide circles, covering over 60 miles (96km).

Indicating just what a positive impression the Bug had made, Lieutenant Colonel Bion J. Arnold, the Army officer in charge of the experiments, ordered seventy-five more devices. He envisioned between 10,000 and 100,000 "flying bombs" being built at a unit cost of $400–$500, but then the Armistice altered the course of events. The Dayton team was disbanded in November 1918, with only a few Bugs completed, although testing did continue after the war—initially at Amityville, Long Island, and later at Carlstrom Field, near Arcadia, Florida. The high missile loss rate continued, however.

All of these early efforts were hampered by the fact that the "flying bombs" were usually designed to undertake but a single flight, terminating in destruction. Building replacements took time and resources, and those investigating the

cause of malfunctions were fortunate indeed if they could find clues in the wreckage. It proved devilishly difficult to design a craft that would fly in a predictable, stable manner without a human pilot, so many were lost on take-off: not surprising when one considers how primitive contemporary aerodynamic research methods were. To make matters worse, the missiles tended

Lawrence Sperry (left), the son of inventor Elmer Sperry, served as a "monitor" pilot aboard the early experimental missiles as a precautionary measure. He was fortunate to escape uninjured when one missile, temporarily fitted with skis, crashed on take-off from the iced-over surface of Great South Bay, Long Island.

to be hastily constructed, and highly fragile, in deference to the "low-cost, throw-away" design philosophy.

At this stage, then, there were few who believed in the practicality of "aerial torpedoes." It would be a long time before technological advancements enabled their true potential to be realized. One key development, in 1922, was the utilization of radio-control equipment. Up until then, the missiles had been designed to fly autonomously, but the prospect of human guidance from afar was a tantalizing one. Although the US Navy had *discussed* radio control as early as 1916, the crucial step of actually employing it was taken not in the United States, but on the other side of the Atlantic, in Great Britain, where substantial progress toward a reliable "flying bomb" had been made.

In May 1919, Britain's Royal Naval Antiaircraft Gunnery Committee had requested a radio-controlled target aircraft. That particular initiative came to nought, but over the next few years the British flew several radio-controlled aircraft as part of a plan to develop a generic "flying bomb"/target missile. They included a Bristol Fighter, a de Havilland

A team which included Orville Wright, created the Kettering Bug. Monitor pilots flew aboard for the initial test flights. Later, the missile took off from a dolly on a rail track, without the aid of a catapult. Sim- *plicity was the keynote: the Bug had no ailerons, and was covered with muslin and brown wrapping paper doped with glycerine and creosote.*

D.H.9A, and a Sperry Avio. The Royal Aircraft Establishment (RAE) developed the 1921 Target aircraft, test-flying it over water in the interests of safety and security from 1922-25. Launched from a catapult device mounted on the deck of a ship, it flew for 39 minutes on its tenth and final test, in March 1925.

Following in the footsteps of the 1921 Target was the smaller, heavier, faster Larynx (Long-Range Gun with Lynx Engine), the product of British efforts to develop a pure "flying bomb." Development was undertaken by the Royal Air Force (RAF) and began in 1925. The first Larynx was lost in the Bristol Channel soon after its catapult launch from HMS *Stronghold* on 25 July 1927. The second Larynx was also destroyed. The third flew 112 miles (179km) at 193mph (309kph), striking the water some 5 miles (8km) from its target. Larynx launches were also conducted from HMS *Thanet*, and from dry land—from Portland, on Britain's south coast—then flight testing was transferred to the Iraqi desert in 1929, with safety and security in mind. In general, the tests were disappointing. Only a small percentage of the flights were successful,

A key development, in 1922, was the utilization of radio-control equipment. The first nation to achieve this was Great Britain, where substantial progress toward a reliable "flying bomb" had been made. This is the Larynx, development of which was undertaken by the Royal Air Force (RAF), prior to a catapult launch from HMS Stronghold.

although much was learnt.

Between the two World Wars, the British only had one successful missile development program: the target missile. Three Fairey IIIF floatplanes were converted to operate by radio control. Known as Fairey Queens, these were followed by a lower-cost target missile— a converted de Havilland Tiger Moth equipped with floats and dubbed the Queen Bee, which first flew under radio control in 1934. Fairey built a total of 420 Queen Bees from 1934-43. (Interestingly, the term "drone"—which is applied to unmanned aircraft to this day—was inspired by the Queen Bee. An early proponent of the "flying bomb," US Navy Lieutenant Commander Delmar S. Fahrney, coined the word in 1936).

Although they weren't direct progenitors of the cruise missile, target missiles played an important role in the development of technologies that would eventually allow "flying bombs" to be fielded operationally.

In America, too, radio control emerged as the best way of improving the accuracy of experimental "flying bombs." Sperry Gyroscope Company, working to a US Army contract, had been offered the unusual incentive of bonus payments for hitting targets. Difficulties with automatic controls in earlier tests involving converted Standard E-1 and Messenger aircraft prompted Lawrence Sperry to install radio-control equipment developed at the Army Engineering Division in 1922. This enabled an operator

Charles Kettering, of Bug fame, developed the General Motors A-1, a radio-controlled monoplane equipped with a 200hp engine and capable of carrying a 500lb (227kg) bomb load 400 miles (640km) at 200mph

(320kph). It made its first flight in 1941, but proved to be little better than "flying bomb" prototypes demonstrated during World War I. In 1943, it was canceled.

seated in a "shepherd" aircraft flying about 1.5 miles (2.4km) away to guide the unmanned device.

By this method, some good results were achieved. Sperry's devices struck their targets twice from a range of 30 miles (48km), three times from 60 miles (96km), and once from 90 miles (144km). Despite protestations from some quarters that employing radio control was contrary to the spirit of the bonus-payment scheme, and that having a shepherd aircraft in close attendance negated the advantages of a stand-off attack, the Army handed Sperry $20,000 in bonuses. The Army proceeded to undertake its own radio-control test program from October 1923 to April 1925, and in 1927 the War Department initiated similar tests, which began in 1929. They were unable to emulate Sperry's successes, however, and progress was further hampered by the economic depression that gripped the nation.

It should be noted that among the Army's proponents of "aerial torpedoes" stood none other than Billy Mitchell, who, in 1923, foresaw the potential benefits of such weapons in the bombardment of battleships, and went on record with this statement: "The aerial torpedo is, and will be, a weapon of tremendous value and terrific force to airpower."

In the mid-1930s, the US Navy's interest in "flying bombs" reawakened. As aforementioned, the Navy was well aware of the advantages they offered, although it had been just beaten to actually flying an aircraft solely by radio control by the British. The Navy had been interested in developing anti-aircraft target missiles, and had initiated a development program through the offices of the Bureau of Ordnance in 1921. Flight tests had begun later that year, but it wasn't until September 1924 that the first successful unmanned,

radio-controlled flight took place. After 1925, budget cuts restricted progress, and efforts to inject fresh impetus into the program some years later were thwarted by further cuts ordered by President Roosevelt in 1933.

The Navy's target missile project rose like the proverbial Phoenix again in 1935, although enthusiasm for it was limited to certain tiny sectors of the service. In February 1937, the device made its first flight, and it served as a gunnery target the following year. By now, the concept of an "assault drone"—an unmanned aircraft with a combat mission—had emerged within the service. A leading proponent of this concept was Lieutenant Commander Fahrney.

The USAAF's wartime chief, General Henry H. (Hap) Arnold, was a firm supporter of the "flying bomb" concept.

13

Two key technologies emerged at this time, assisting the development of such a missile. One was television, the other the radar altimeter. Television, demonstrated by RCA in 1937 as a means of enhancing airborne reconnaissance, provided a means of extending the "sight" of an operator remotely-controlling an unmanned aircraft—so long as the drone remained within radio range, of course. The radar altimeter was equally advantageous, offering a means by which an unmanned aircraft could maintain a low altitude over uneven terrain. In 1941, the Navy successfully flight-tested a drone equipped with a radar altimeter.

Technological breakthroughs aside, progress was slow. Tests of target drones simulating assault drones took place in September 1940, but it was not until November 1941 that the Chief of the Bureau of Aeronautics issued the order for 100 obsolescent torpedo bombers to be converted into assault drones and a further 100 missiles to be purpose-designed for the same role. Then the Japanese attacked Pearl Harbor, and the Navy immediately reclaimed the 100 torpedo bombers for training purposes.

Despite these setbacks, the Navy did undertake two significant demonstrations in April 1942 (involving two different types of drones: a TG-2 and a BG-1). Both involved launching a TV-equipped, torpedo-toting drone from its parent vessel and radio-controlling it in a simulated attack on another ship. The Bureau of Aeronautics placed an order for 200 drones that month. That order was increased to 1,000 the following month, but then came opposition. With America now comprehensively engaged in World War II, why should huge

The only USAAF "flying bomb" employed in combat during World War II was the BQ-7 Aphrodite. War-weary Boeing B-17 Flying Fortress bombers, one of which is seen here, stripped of their armament and other un-wanted equipment, were loaded with 18,500lb (8,340kg) of explosive and flown by radio control to targets in Germany. At cruising altitude, the crew of two parachuted to safety over English soil.

Although the earliest efforts to develop a practical "flying bomb" had taken place in the United States and Britain, it was in Germany that a workable concept finally emerged. Although crude by today's stan- *dards, the V-1 "Revenge Weapon" was employed to devastating effect in World War II, when it was unleashed against British and other European cities, claiming thousands of lives.*

resources be directed toward a weapon that was still, for the most part, unproven? The Chief of the Bureau of Aeronautics, John H. Towers—generally considered to be the "father" of naval aviation—was opposed to the "flying bomb" concept and recommended cutting the order to 500 missiles. This recommendation was approved in August 1942.

Although the Navy examined increasing the order to as much as 3,000 drones the following year, circumstances were not in favor of it. Difficulties abounded. The contractor, Interstate Aircraft and Engineering, could not produce the drones rapidly enough, and a structural defect was revealed following the crash of one drone. Another high-powered opponent of the "flying bomb" was also vociferous in his criticism of the weapon: the Commander of the Pacific Fleet, Admiral Chester W. Nimitz. It should not be forgotten that the develop-

ment of the "flying bomb" was hindered not only by the technological limitations of the day, but also by the barriers of apathy, ignorance, and even downright hostility on occasion. In March 1944, the Navy cut its overall order to 388 missiles: the 100 Interstate TDNs already accepted, plus 188 TDR-1s, fifty TDR2Rs, and fifty TD3Rs.

Finally, in 1944, the Navy conducted combat tests of the assault drones, though not before a Japanese merchant ship beached at Cape Esperance had been employed as an impromptu target (the drones achieved two direct hits and two near misses). In the combat tests themselves, twenty-nine out of forty-six TDR drones launched reached their targets, three having fallen prey to Japanese antiaircraft fire, and others to a variety of technical problems. This made no great impression in the corridors of power, and funding was cut off even before the last missile had been fired, around 200 having been delivered up to that point. The program was offered, lock, stock, and barrel, to the Army Air Forces (AAF), but was declined.

The AAF was not entirely opposed to the "flying bomb." Indeed, its wartime chief, General Henry H. (Hap) Arnold, was a firm supporter of the concept. But the AAF had its own ideas as to how such a weapon should be developed, and these had come to focus on the efforts of Charles Kettering, of Bug fame. The Army ordered ten examples of a new-type "flying bomb" from Kettering's company, General Motors, in February 1941. This was the General Motors A-1, a radio-controlled monoplane equipped with a 200hp engine and capable of carrying a 500lb (227kg) bomb load 400

miles (640km) at 200mph (320kph). Initial tests took place at Langley Field, Virginia, then four A-1s were flight tested by the Army at the Lake Muroc dry lakebed site in southern California. Like its predecessor, the Bug, the A-1 was launched from a dolly mounted on a length of rail track. The early flights were unsatisfactory, and modifications were ordered, including provision for altitude control and the incorporation of a power catapult.

Flight tests resumed at Eglin Field, Florida. One GM A-1 flew for 1 hour, 40 minutes on 2 April 1941, but poor directional control was noted. There were other problems in store. Army aviators expressed concern that the A-1's bomb load might prove insufficient, and were

When northern France was liberated, denying the Germans their V-1 launching sites close to British soil, the Luftwaffe resorted to air-launching the missiles from Heinkel He 111 medium bombers. This allowed targets as far afield as Manchester to become V-1 targets.

unhappy about its reliance on a shepherd aircraft. General Motors proposed a twin-engined version, which could carry a much larger bomb load much further. However, aero-engines were in short supply in wartime America, as elsewhere, so that solution was unworkable. Further modifications were made to the remaining A-1s, but they continued to be claimed by accidents.

Probably more in desperation than anything else, air-launching was considered. The North American B-25 seemed a suitable "mother" aircraft, and the Army conducted a series of wind-tunnel tests at Wright Field, Ohio, to verify the effectiveness of the combination. This concept was not pursued, however. The A-1's final flight took place at Lake Muroc in 1943, it having been concluded that the time and money required to develop it into an operational asset could be better spent elsewhere. The A-1 program had cost the Army around $350,000.

The AAF only employed one "flying bomb" in combat during World War II: the BQ-7 Aphrodite, based on the Boeing B-17 Flying Fortress bomber. War-weary B-17s were stripped of their armament and other unwanted equipment, then loaded with 18,500lb (8,340kg) of explosive. They were flown from conventional runways in England by a human pilot who remained aboard until he had taken the aircraft to cruising altitude, at which point an electrical technician made necessary adjustments to the radio-control equipment and activated the explosive fuze. Both crewmembers then parachuted to safety over English soil, leaving an operator in a shepherd aircraft to guide the airplane-turned-missile (trailing white smoke to aid identification) to its target.

Early attempts to launch Aphrodites against German targets were fraught with difficulties. The first mission took place on 4 August 1944 and failed, setting an unfortunate trend. In an attempt to improve accuracy, television equipment was installed aboard Aphrodites, but they continued to fall prey to German fighters and antiaircraft fire. A planned campaign of Aphrodite attacks against German cities fizzled out.

The Navy undertook a similar airplane-turned-missile conversion, employing another four-engined heavy bomber, the Consolidated B-24 Liberator. The unmanned B-24, designated BQ-8, was fitted with a different radio-control system to that installed aboard the AAF's Aphrodite BQ-7, and also carried a television sensor. The first trial took place on 12 August 1944, and ended disastrously when the weapon blew up, killing Navy Lieutenants Wilford J. Willy and Joseph P. Kennedy, Jr. (the brother of future United States President John F. Kennedy). Later that day, a second mission destroyed some German facilities at Heligoland, but not the intended target, as there was poor TV image reception. That marked the end of this particular experiment.

Although the earliest efforts to develop a practical "flying bomb" had taken place in the United States and Britain, it was in Germany that a workable concept finally emerged. Although crude by today's standards, the fruits of Germany's efforts were demonstrated to devastating effect in World War II, when V-1 "flying bombs" were unleashed against British and other European cities, claiming thousands of lives. Officially designated the Fieseler Fi 103 (FZG-76), but more popularly known in Germany as the *Vergeltungswaffe 1* (Revenge Weapon 1), it weighed 4,750lb (2,165kg) in operational form, of which about 1,870lb (850kg) constituted the high-explosive warhead.

German experimentation with the "flying bomb" concept had begun in the 1930s, when two companies, Askania and Siemens, conducted some preliminary research. It was an independent inventor who made the most significant progress, however. Paul Schmidt, who had patented a pulsejet engine in 1931, teamed with G. Madelung in 1934 to propose a pulsejet-powered "flying bomb." A development contract followed, and four years later an unmanned bomber was demonstrated to the Luftwaffe. There was a great deal of interest in the weapon, but no production contract resulted, because it was deemed deficient with respect to range and accuracy, and there were concerns about the cost of developing an operational version.

When Germany captured France in 1940, it opened up the possibility of launching "flying bombs" against Britain. With London and several other major British cities—Southampton, for example —so close at hand, a reliable radio-control system would no longer be a prerequisite to success. Adolf Hitler, incensed by the relentless bombing of German cities, sought a new weapon with which to wreak revenge on the British people (yet it had been Germany that first introduced the concept of aerial bombardment of civilian populations in cities, during the Spanish Civil War). The Luftwaffe hierarchy was equally enthusiastic about obtaining a weapon that would match the destructive potential of the German Army's V-2 ballistic missile, then under development.

In June 1942, the Luftwaffe accorded top priority to a teaming of three German companies tasked with developing and mass-producing an effective "flying bomb" from readily-available, low-cost materials. The companies in question were Fieseler, supplying the airframe, Argus (for which

Paul Schmidt now worked), supplying the pulsejet, and Askania, supplying the guidance system. The hastily-developed new weapon made its first flight—a glide test from a Focke-Wulf Fw 200 Condor long-range maritime bomber aircraft—that December. On Christmas Eve, it made its first boosted flight.

On 26 May 1943, key Nazi leaders travelled to the V-1 test facility at Peenemünde, situated on a tongue of land on Germany's Baltic coast, to assess progress. A decision was made to enter full-scale production, and by July the V-1 was demonstrating its ability to impact within 0.5-mile (0.8-km) of its aim point after a flight of 152 miles (243km). The V-1 was launched from a long ramp with the aid of a hydrogen peroxide/potassium permanganate-propelled booster motor. This accelerated it to 200mph (320kph): a necessary measure, because the V-1's Argus 109-014 pulsejet could not function at speeds below 150mph (240kph). The pulsejet developed 600lb (2,670kN) of thrust. A gyroscope, a magnetic compass and a barometric altimeter guided the missile to its target.

With its fuel load depleted, shortly prior to impact, the V-1 could travel at approximately 400mph (640kph). At a preset point in the flight, the control surfaces locked and spoilers deployed from the tail to induce a steep dive. At this point the pulsejet usually ceased functioning, the eerie silence heralding the impending impact.

Well over 10,000 V-1s were launched against Britain, in all weathers, by day and night. Despite heavy Allied bombing of the V-1 test facilities at Peenemünde and numerous V-1 launching sites in northwestern France, vigorous anti-aircraft fire from radar-assisted coastal and city defenses, and barrage balloon protection, many V-1s got through to their targets. On one particularly harrowing occasion, on 18 June 1944, a V-1 struck the chapel at Wellington Barracks, only a short distance from Buckingham Palace, killing 119 worshippers and injuring a further 141. Later, attacks against V-1 production and storage facilities had more effect, and RAF fighter pilots had some success in shooting them down, though they had to take care to avoid the V-1's exhaust plume when closing in on it, as well as avoiding the flying debris if a hit was scored.

Later still, RAF pilots developed a method of "tipping" V-1s out of control by making wingtip-to-wingtip contact: the sudden movement destabilized the missile's gyroscope. Only the fastest Allied fighters—Supermarine Spitfire Mk.14s, Hawker Tempest Mk.5s, North American Mustang 3s, and de Havilland Mosquito Mk.13s—could keep up with the speeding missiles. When Britain's Gloster Meteor,

the Allies' only jet fighter to see action in World War II, entered service in July 1944, its first operational duty was to attack V-1s.

When northern France was liberated, denying the Germans their V-1 launching sites close to British soil, the Luftwaffe resorted to air-launching the missiles from Heinkel He 111 medium bombers. This allowed targets as far afield as Manchester to become V-1 targets. The Germans found another way to extend their reach, by developing an increased-range version of the V-1. It had a lighter wing, made of wood instead of metal, and a smaller, lighter warhead, allowing it to fly about 220 miles (350km), as compared to the 150-160 miles (240-256km) of the standard V-1.

It should not be forgotten that at least 7,400 V-1s, and possibly as many as 9,000, were launched against targets in mainland Europe—particularly the vital

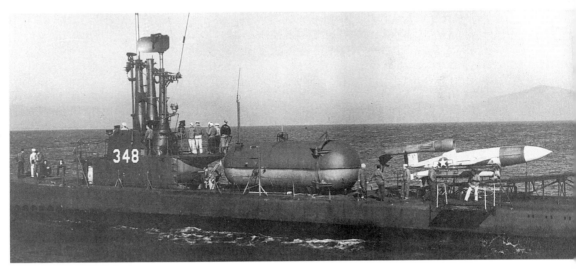

America built its own version of the V-1, initially by using a large batch of captured German parts air-freighted from Britain to Wright-Patterson Field in July 1944. The Army copy was designated JB-2, while the Navy version—shown here—was known as the Loon. This Loon is about to be launched from a ramp on the deck of the submarine USS Cusk, *in November 1948.*

Belgian port of Antwerp and the nearby city of Liege. A total of about 30,000 V-1s had been produced by the time Germany capitulated. True, the weapon had its limitations. Although—being small and fast-flying—it presented a difficult target for antiaircraft gunners and Allied fighters to hit, it was launched from fixed facilities against known targets, so defenses could be readily concentrated against it. While it was certainly more accurate than previous "flying bombs" over such distances, it was only able to impact at random within the perimeters of large cities, as opposed to striking specific targets. It was therefore more of a "terror weapon" than a genuine threat to the Allies' ability to wage war. Nevertheless, it showed the way forward—and the Americans, in particular, took heed.

In fact, the Americans built their own version of the V-1. A large batch of captured V-1 parts was air-freighted from Britain to Wright-Patterson Field in July 1944, the intention being to assemble thirteen copies. It took just three weeks for the AAF to build the first: the Army copies were designated JB-2. Plans took shape to improve on the

While flight-testing its V-1 copy, the Army also evaluated the futuristic-looking Northrop JB-1. It was originally powered by a pair of turbojets, but these developed insuf- *ficient thrust, so it was re-engined with a pulsejet and redesignated JB-10. This JB-10 is being readied for flight at Eglin Air Force Base, Florida, in April 1945.*

accuracy of the V-1. An order for 1,000 all-new JB-2s was placed in August, with Republic contracted to supply the airframes, Ford the engines, Jack and Heinz the control system, and Alloy Products the pressure vessels. Contracts were also awarded to Monsanto, for launch rockets, and Northrop, for launch sleds.

While the war in the Pacific raged, enthusiasm for the "flying bomb" ran high in certain quarters of the AAF. Army flight testing of the JB-2 included air-launching trials, with a B-17 serving as the mother aircraft. In January 1945, the service increased its order for JB-2s to an incredible 75,000! It was felt that the JB-2 could serve as a useful weapon on days when poor weather conditions prevented manned aircraft from striking at targets. On the other side of the debate, there were those who felt that the apportioning of precious resources to a major "flying bomb" production program might adversely effect other elements of the American war effort. By the end of January, the War Department had decided not to proceed with mass production of the JB-2.

Within weeks, this decision looked like it would be overturned, as plans evolved for a more manageable production run. The Japanese surrender changed all that, and when JB-2 production ended in September 1945, just under 1,400 had been delivered. The V-1 story doesn't end there, however, because after the war, the Navy, which had also been involved in assessing the German weapon, conducted launches of its own version, known as the Loon. The first of these launches took place on 7 January 1946, and the first launch from the deck of a surfaced submarine—the USS *Cusk* —took place on 18 February 1947.

While the JB-2 effort was under way, the Army was running another "flying bomb" program. The missile, built

by Northrop, was designated JB-1, and was intended to carry two 2,000lb (910kg) bombs, 200 miles (320km) at speeds in excess of 400mph (640kph). However, the original powerplants, a pair of General Electric B1 turbojets, were found to be developing insufficient thrust, complicating what had already become a fraught test program. To remedy the lack of thrust, Northrop obtained some pulsejets from the JB-2 program and built a revised airframe around the new engine. The re-engined missile was designated JB-10, and carried two slightly lighter bombs. Flight testing resumed, but the writing was on the wall. By general consensus, Northrop had over-engineered the JB-1/JB-10— building a missile to aircraft standards, with the attendant cost escalation— and in March 1946, the futuristic-looking device joined the long list of canceled projects.

The immediate postwar period was a time of great change, characterized by the descoping of military capabilities and much jostling-for-position between the various military services. In 1947, the airmen of the US Army gained their long-awaited independence: the USAAF became the US Air Force (USAF). There was a proliferation of guided missiles in the United States' arsenal at that time, but the number was slashed by budget cuts the following year. In 1946, it had been suggested that the AAF develop a guided missile with a range of at least 1,000 miles (1,600km) to further the cause of the "flying bomb" concept. The result was the Banshee, an unpiloted version of the Boeing B-29 Superfortress heavy bomber. This variation on the theme so thoroughly discredited by the earlier Aphrodite program also failed dismally, and the project was canceled in April 1949.

Other ventures fared somewhat

better, though the hoped-for break-throughs in accuracy and reliability were a long time in coming. One missile, in particular, highlighted the frustrations of this phase in the development of the cruise missile. The Northrop Snark was the product of a wartime AAF require-ment for a 600mph (960km) surface-to-surface missile with a range of 5,000 miles (8,000km). Northrop responded by proposing a turbojet-powered missile with a range little more than half that, and landed a research contract as a result. Jack Northrop himself coined the name Snark, borrowing from the works of Lewis Carroll. For a time, the Snark program was an on-off affair, but even-tually the missile was built. In December 1950, the first attempt at launching a Snark failed. It was several months before the first success, after which the duration of the test flights was increased to a

The Northrop Snark. The initial version—shown here—was designated N25, was larger and heavier than previous "flying bombs," and far superior in performance terms. For guidance over intercontinental distances, an inertial navigation system monitored by stellar navigation was envisaged. A proto-type system, weighing almost 1 ton (910kg), was flight-tested.

maximum of 2 hours, 46 minutes.

The initial Snark variant, designated N25, was powered by a single Allison J33 turbojet. It was larger and heavier than previous "flying bombs," and far superior in performance terms, with a cruising speed of Mach 0.85 over 1,550 miles (2,480km). The N25 did not have hor- izontal stabilizers, and had elevons instead of conventional ailerons and elevators. It was controlled in flight by a specially-equipped North American B-45 Tornado light bomber serving as a shepherd aircraft, and was equipped with retractable skids and a drag para- chute for horizontal landings. Flight

A Snark and a Northrop F-89 in formation in October 1956. The F-89 is serving as a shepherd aircraft, controlling the Snark in flight. Note the Snark's retractable skid landing gear.

Spectacular firing of a Snark from a mobile launch platform. This particular variant was designated SM-62: the initials stood for Strategic Missile. It was the operational version of the N-69E "Super Snark," pro-duced in response to USAF demands for even greater performance. The two booster rockets are clearly visible, as is the distinctive "saw tooth" wing shape.

testing was conducted at Holloman Air Force Base, New Mexico. The N-25s were sled-launched. For guidance over intercontinental distances, an inertial navigation system monitored by stellar navigation was envisaged, and a prototype system —weighing almost 1 ton (910kg)—was flight-tested aboard a variety of aircraft. Northrop claimed that this system would enable an average of 50 percent of Snarks launched to impact within a 1.6-mile (2.59-km) radius following a flight to maximum range: sufficient accuracy for a nuclear-tipped missile.

A "Super Snark" variant, designated N-69, was produced in response to Air Force demands for even greater performance. It was larger than the N-25, featured a distinctive "saw tooth" wing, had a more powerful engine (the J71, and later the J57), and was assisted into the air by two booster rockets. Flight testing was switched to the Atlantic Missile Range in Florida in 1952, disrupting the program considerably. The N-69 was dogged by problems. Flight testing, conducted from Patrick Air Force Base, revealed excessive fuel consumption, then an even more serious problem emerged: there was inadequate elevon control during the terminal dive into the target. In July 1955, to circumvent this problem, the Air Force agreed to a revised attack mode in which the missile's nose section, which would contain the warhead, would separate before impact and fly a ballistic trajectory to the target.

Many flight tests ended well short of their destinations. In fact, N-69 crashes into the Atlantic Ocean became so frequent that a particular region just off the Florida coast was wryly referred to as "Snark-infested waters." Other Snark flights went to the opposite extreme. Control would be lost, and the missiles would fly off on their own, disappearing into the distance. One Snark that went

missing in December 1956 was not found until a farmer happened across it in a Brazilian jungle in 1982!

Flight testing continued, and despite the overwhelming evidence of inaccuracy and unreliability, and growing concern about its vulnerability to enemy defenses, in May 1959 the first Snark was delivered to the newly-activated 702nd Strategic Missile Wing at Presque Isle, Maine: designated as the USAF's first operational Snark unit. In February 1961, the Snark was finally declared operational, but its period of service was to be a short one. The Snark had only been operational for a matter of weeks when a newly-incumbent President John F. Kennedy canceled the whole program, citing the missile's inferiority to ballistic missiles among a long list of criticisms.

A similar fate befell the more spectacular and ambitious Navaho program, which ran concurrently with the Snark effort. The North American Navaho was a two-element, "piggy-back" device inspired, at least in part, by German World War II technology. A turbojet-powered missile element was carried aloft on the back of a rocket-powered booster vehicle, in order to facilitate intercontinental flight distances at supersonic speeds (the Snark was subsonic). In its initial, test-specification form, the missile element, designated X-10, was flown independently. The X-10 was powered by two Westinghouse J40WE-1 turbojets, was 70ft (21m) long, had a delta wing measuring 28ft (8.5m), and had canard control surfaces on its nose and a distinctive V-shaped tail. It was radio-controlled and had a retractable undercarriage. Eleven X-10s flew a total of twenty-seven times. A maximum speed of Mach 2.05 was attained, setting a new world record for turbojet-powered aircraft.

An interim-specification version of

the missile element, designated XSM-64, was similar in size and configuration to the X-10, but was powered by two Curtiss-Wright RJ47 ramjet engines. It was carried on the back of a huge rocket booster element producing 415,000lb (1,846,000kN) of thrust, and measuring 76 ft, 3in (23m) in length. The mated combination measured 82ft, 5in (25m) in length, and was launched vertically: as spectacular a sight as any in aviation history up to that time. Unfortunately, the Navaho's visual impact was not matched by its performance. It was found to be riddled with gremlins, and soon earned the epithet "Never go, Navaho."

In July 1957, only months after the XSM-64's first flight, the Navaho program was canceled. It proved overly ambitious to build a missile capable of self-navigating for many hours, over distances of up to 5,000 miles (8,000km). The emerging generation of ballistic missiles, epitomized by the Convair Atlas, which first flew in June 1957, looked a surer bet. They could reach their targets far quicker, and were immune to enemy defensive fire. The Air Force authorized five more Navaho flights to make the most of the surviving hardware. On one of these flights, a speed in excess of Mach 3 was attained. Two additional flights took place in the closing months of 1958, as part of the Research In Supersonic Environment (RISE) program, and there it ended.

If there was a positive aspect to the Navaho program—which had cost the American taxpayer over $700 million, yet yielded less than 1.5 hours of flying time—it was the advancement of certain critical technologies. Among them were ramjet propulsion, autonavigation, canard control, and high-thrust-level rocket boost. These technologies found applications in a host of subsequent aviation,

space, and even maritime programs (when the USS *Nautilus* undertook her historic below-ice passage of the North Pole, she did so with a navigation system derived from that developed for the Navaho).

In addition to the Snark and the Navaho, there was a third significant USAF-sponsored cruise missile of the 1940s/1950s era: the Martin company's Matador. Martin designed the Matador in response to a 1945 AAF requirement for a 600mph (960kph) surface-to-surface missile with a range of 175-500 miles (280-800km). When it finally emerged, the missile could better that performance—although not dependably. It was boosted from its mobile launcher by a jettisonable rocket motor capable of developing 57,000lb (253,500kN) of thrust for a period of 2.4 seconds: sufficient to accelerate the missile to a flying speed of 200mph (320kph).

The Matador was smaller than the Snark, weighed 12,000lb (5,450kg), was powered by an Allison J33-A-37 turbojet developing 4,600lb (20,460kN) of thrust, and carried a 3,000lb (1,360kg) warhead. It made its first flight on 19 January 1949. Forty-six prototype Matadors were succeeded by eighty-four production examples, all designated TM-61A, then a further batch of Matadors was introduced, with strengthened wings and tail units. Both of these variants were controlled by a ground-based operator employing a radar tracking system, but this limited the Matador's range to "line-of-sight" communication: about 250 miles (400km). The USAF added a guidance system called Shanicle in late 1954, and missiles thus equipped were redesignated TM-61Cs. Shanicle-equipped Matadors were still limited to "line-of-sight" transmissions, but they were more accurate. Test flights conducted at the Atlantic Missile Range indicated that 50

The North American Navaho was an awesome, two-element, "piggy-back" device. A turbojet-powered missile element was carried aloft on the back of a rocket-powered booster vehicle, to facilitate intercontinental flight distances at supersonic speeds. In its initial, test-specification form, the missile element, designated X-10—seen here—was flown independently. From October 1953, eleven X-10s flew a total of twenty-seven times. One set a new world speed record for turbojet-powered aircraft.

27

percent of TM-61Cs launched could be expected to impact within 1,600ft (490m) of a specific aim point.

To overcome the Matador's reliance on "line-of-sight" communications, the USAF installed a radar terrain-matching system aboard the TM-61B variant of the Matador, which was known as the Mace, in 1952. Radar terrain-matching is a navigation method based on the "fingerprint" principle: namely, that no two land surfaces are exactly the same. By matching the contours of hills, gullies and other features with a series of profiles stored in its computer, a missile could navigate with great accuracy. The difficulty was in achieving this capability with the limited technology of the day.

In 1952, the TM-61B variant of the Martin Matador, known as the Mace, was fitted with a radar terrain-matching system. This was a significant development, because it foreshadowed the incorporation of a highly-evolved derivative system in today's Tomahawk. Here, a Mace blasts away from its launch apparatus.

The radar terrain-matching system installed in the TM-61B Mace was the first of its type: Goodyear Aircraft's Automatic Terrain Recognition and Navigation (ATRAN) system, first laboratory tested in March 1948. The TM-61B differed substantially from its sisters, the A- and C-variant Matadors. It had a longer fuselage, shorter wings, more weight, more booster thrust, more cruise engine thrust, and it cost considerably more. The differences were so numerous that the USAF eventually assigned the B-variant Matador a totally separate designation: TM-76A. Highlighting its freedom from "line-of-sight" communications, the Mace had a range of 540 miles (865km) at low level, and 1,285 miles (2,055km) at high altitude.

Like the Snark, Matadors and Maces saw operational service. By the time the Mace made its first flight, TM-61A Matadors had been enjoying operational status in West Germany for over a year with the 1st Pilotless Bomber Squadron. TM-61C Matadors became operational with the 58th Tactical Missile Group in South Korea in January 1959. Maces were stationed at USAF facilities in Europe from 1959 to 1969, and on the Japanese island of Okinawa, with the 498th Tactical Missile Group, from 1961 to 1969.

The conferral of operational status on the Matador and Mace should not be taken as evidence of their efficacy. They suffered from all manner of problems, and they were certainly not ready to enter service when they did. Firings in

Florida and Libya demonstrated poor accuracy and low reliability, and there were concerns about their limited mobility (twenty-eight different vehicles were required to support the Matador).

While the USAF was pursuing the Snark, Navaho and Matador/Mace programs, the Navy had been zealously guarding its own position in the guided missile field with a missile very similar to the Matador—indeed, powered by the same engine: the J33 turbojet. Known as the Regulus, it was developed by Chance Vought as an outgrowth of a study contract awarded to the company back in 1943. By August 1947, the Navy's performance requirements had been

refined. The missile would have to carry a 3,000lb (1,360kg) warhead up to 575 miles (920km) at Mach 0.85. Accuracy requirements were such that 50 percent of Regulus firings would be expected to impact within one mile (1.6km) of a specific aim point for every 200 miles (320km) flown.

A key factor in the development of the Regulus was the Navy's desire to delivery a nuclear warhead. In the late 1940s, atomic warheads typically weighed about five tons (4,550kg): too heavy for most carrier-based aircraft. As the Regulus program matured, the Navy successfully avoiding project cancelation or amalgamation by persuading

A Mace jettisons its booster rocket. Maces were stationed at USAF facilities in Europe from 1959 to 1969, and on the Japanese island of Okinawa, with the 498th Tactical Missile Group, from 1961 to 1969.

the Department of Defense (DoD) that its specific requirements were sufficiently different from the Air Force's to necessitate a missile similar, but not identical to, the latter's Matador.

The Regulus made its first flight in March 1951. It undertook its first submarine launch, from the deck of the USS *Tunny*, in July 1953. At launch, the missile was boosted aloft by two rocket motors, each developing 33,000lb (146,800kN) of thrust. It was then radio-controlled to its target by operators in two submerged submarines stationed along the route. In 1955, the Regulus was declared operational, and served aboard a variety of submarines and surface vessels. It was withdrawn from service in 1964, some say prematurely.

A follow-on missile for the Navy—the Grumman Rigel, powered by a Marquardt ramjet—proved extremely

The US Navy's Chance Vought Regulus was boosted aloft by two rocket motors, each developing 33,000lb (146,800kN) of thrust, then radio-controlled to its target by operators in two submerged submarines stationed along the route. In 1955, the Regulus was declared operational, and served aboard a variety of submarines and surface vessels. It was withdrawn from service in 1964, some say prematurely. This Regulus is being launched from the submarine USS Halibut (SSGN-587) in March 1960.

troublesome, and that program was canceled in August 1953. The "original" Regulus was therefore replaced by the Regulus 2, a supersonic version with canard control surfaces on the nose. The Regulus 2 undertook its maiden flight in April 1955, and the first launch from a surface vessel (the USS *King County*) took place in December 1958. Only one submarine launch took place: from the USS *Grayback* in September 1958.

The Regulus 2 program was canceled that December, when Chance Vought had completed only twenty examples. The reasons cited were high cost (the missiles cost $1 million apiece) and the fact that the smaller, more powerful, new-generation nuclear weapons then emerging could be more reliably delivered by conventional aircraft launched by steam catapults from the slanted decks of Naval carriers. The steam catapult and the slanted deck were just being introduced into the Navy at this time, allowing heavier, higher-performance jet aircraft to be carrier-launched.

In this summary of the evolution of the cruise missile, several other guided weapons are worthy of mention. One was the Radioplane Crossbow, developed in the early 1950s in response to a USAF requirement for an air-to-surface missile capable of homing on and destroying enemy ground radar installations. The intention was to launch Crossbows out of enemy radar range from heavy bomber aircraft of the Strategic Air Command (SAC): at least four missiles per aircraft, slung from underwing pylons. The Crossbow had an estimated range of 290 miles (465km). After launch from 34,000ft (10,370m), it would climb to 40,000ft (12,200m) and transit to the target area at 540mph (865kph). When it was about 7 miles (11.2km) from the target radar installation, the Crossbow would make a 30-degree power dive onto it.

Designated GAM-67, the Crossbow made its first powered flight during a test program conducted at Holloman Air Force Base in March 1956. The first guided flight took place in May of the following year. Although the Crossbow demonstrated a high degree of accuracy, it met its demise on a combination of financial grounds and performance deficiencies (it proved unable to achieve its design speed, and had insufficient range to evade Soviet radar).

Another weapon significant to cruise missile development at this time was the North American Hound Dog, which owed its name to the Elvis Presley hit! It was an inertially-guided, air-to-surface missile developed partly to increase the number of US strategic weapons, and partly to reduce the dependency on manned penetrating bombers in situations where they would prove vulnerable to enemy defenses. The Hound Dog grew from a USAF requirement tabled in 1956, and was initially designated GAM-77, but later redesignated AGM-28. It was powered by a Pratt & Whitney J52 ramjet mounted on a short pylon beneath the belly. Its other distinctive features were a delta wing, and canard control surfaces on the nose.

Two of these five-ton (4,550-kg) missiles were carried by the Boeing B-52 heavy bomber on underwing pylons. Flight crews learned that they could shorten the B-52's takeoff roll by using the Hound Dog's engines to augment the overall thrust level (they then replenished the missiles from the bomber's own fuel tanks). This was the only performance gain, however. The extra weight and drag of the two Hound Dogs significantly reduced the B-52's climbing and cruising capabilities.

The Hound Dog became operational in July 1961, and the total number on strength peaked at 593 two years later. In AGM-28B form, it toted a 1,742lb (790kg) warhead, and could fly 750 miles (1,200km) at a speed of Mach 2 and an altitude of over 55,000ft (16,780m), or alternatively fly 390 miles (625km) at Mach 0.83 in a low-level regime. At maximum range, it could generally be expected to impact a little over 1 mile (1.6km) from its aim point. Given the fact that it carried a 4-megaton warhead, this would have been sufficiently accurate.

Dwindling numbers of Hound Dogs served into the next decade, and the weapon was finally phased out of service in 1976, to be replaced by an air-launched ballistic missile: the smaller, lighter, faster Short-Range Attack Missile (SRAM).

A breed of guided missile known as the "decoy missile" is another important strand in our story—even though such devices had a non-offensive role—because the experience gained in designing, building and operating them was put to good use in the advancement of the cruise missile. Decoy missiles emerged in the United States in the 1950s. They were designed to confuse the enemy by creating the same radar signature as USAF bombers. Enemy defenses would be diluted by such subterfuge, increasing the effectiveness of an attack by manned penetrating bombers.

The Consolidated-Vultee Buck Duck was intended to be the USAF's first operational decoy missile, but glide tests in early 1955 do not appear to have given way to powered trials before the program was canceled in January of the following year. The plan had been for

Following cancellation of the troublesome Grumman Rigel, the Navy replaced the "original" Regulus with the Regulus 2, a supersonic version with canard control surfaces on the nose. The Regulus 2 undertook its maiden flight in April 1955, and its first launch from a surface vessel—seen here—took place from the USS King County *in December 1958.*

six Buck Ducks to be carried by the Convair B-36 heavy bomber, but by this time the Boeing B-52 Stratofortress was about to emerge as its replacement, so the Buck Duck's period of service would have been unacceptably short.

Fairchild's Bull Goose fared little better. Designated XSM-73, it was a ground-launched decoy missile with intercontinental range. It had a delta wing and was boosted from its launcher by a rocket motor developing 50,000lb (222,400kN) of thrust. The Bull Goose

made its first flight in June 1957, in the Atlantic Test Range. In trials, it proved incapable of simulating the B-52 on radar screens. That, as well as mounting budgetary pressures, forced the Bull Goose's cancelation in December 1958, although the USAF did considered arming it.

Only one decoy missile stands out with distinction: McDonnell's GAM-72 Quail. Not only did it achieve operational status, it also served for more than a decade. The Quail emerged from a USAF

Two five-ton (4,550-kg) Hound Dogs were carried by the Boeing B-52 heavy bomber on *underwing pylons, as seen in this photo, taken in 1961.*

requirement first expressed in 1952, but not formally defined until 1956. Designed to operate at altitudes of 35,000-50,000ft (10,670-15,250m), at speeds of Mach 0.75-0.9, over distances of at least 300 miles (480km), it was powered by a single General Electric J85 turbojet—the same engine that powers the Northrop T-38 trainer. Its first powered flight took place in August 1958.

Quails were air-launched from SAC B-52s and Boeing B-47s. The B-52 was capable of carrying eight Quails, while the B-47 could carry four, but in both cases the aircraft usually carried only half that quantity. The Quail had a slab-sided fuselage and four vertical stabilizers, all helping to produce a radar signature similar to that of the B-52. Its flight performance was comparable to the B-52, and it could be pre-programmed to undertake at least two changes in direction and one in speed, making it appear more like a manned aircraft to radar observers. To add to the subterfuge, the Quail was equipped with a small electronic countermeasures (ECM) package that could provide a heat source and dispense chaff.

McDonnell produced a total of 616 Quails. At the pinnacle of its period of service with SAC, in 1963, there were 492 in inventory. By the early 1970s, however, it had outlived its usefulness. Advances in Soviet radar made it a relatively easy task to distinguish a Quail from a genuine B-52.

It is fair to say that the overall record of unmanned aircraft up to this point was not an illustrious one. Technology ranging from the unproven to the unworkable had kept such weapons firmly in the "second league" to manned aircraft. As we shall see, in the 1960s, enormous advances in technology changed that situation, and the cruise missile could at long last emerge as a contender.

Chapter 2

Birth of the Tomahawk

The Technological Leap

When the 1970s began, the "flying bomb" concept had still to make a *niche* for itself. Up to that time, the weapons we now classify as cruise missiles were, by and large, cumbersome, unreliable, and inaccurate. Not surprisingly, therefore, the military mainstream regarded them with scepticism and suspicion. Then came the Tomahawk: compact, able to achieve a hit rate in excess of 90 percent, and accurate to within a matter of feet. How did this transformation come about?

The answer as to how a small, reliable, and highly-accurate weapon like the Tomahawk sprang from earlier weapons that were none of these things lies in a combination of technological advancement and accumulated operational experience. The key factors that facilitated this technological leap can be itemized as follows:

■ Burgeoning advances in guidance system technology and computing power. In the 1950s and 1960s, the physical dimensions of inertial guidance systems reduced markedly, their weight diminished by a similarly spectacular degree, their electrical power requirements shrank, and their accuracy improved exponentially. Added to this were enormous strides in computer technology, in respect both to size and capability, and the refinement of radar terrain-matching systems.

We noted, in Chapter 1, that the first radar terrain-matching system, Goodyear Aircraft's ATRAN, was installed in the USAF's Martin TM-61B Mace, in order to overcome the limitations of its Shanicle guidance system. A development of ATRAN was to have been installed in what was termed, in 1955, "the ultimate cruise missile," the Mach 3.5 Triton, with its phenomenal range of 13,800 miles (22,080km). However, key technological advances in naval aviation —particularly the emergence of the steam catapult and the slanted deck on US Navy aircraft carriers, facilitating the operation of heavier and higher-performing jets—resulted in conventional manned aircraft remaining at the fore, so the Triton never got beyond the full-scale development stage.

In 1958, the LTV-Electro Systems Company (later to become E-Systems) patented a similar, but more capable, system that brought a new acronym to military aviation: TERCOM (*Terrain Contour Matching*). TERCOM was to have served as a key element in the guidance system for Chance Vought's Supersonic Low-Altitude Missile (SLAM). Although SLAM was canceled in 1959, TERCOM lived on.

A detailed description of how TERCOM works can be found in Chapter 4. Here, it suffices to say that TERCOM evolved into an exceptionally capable navigation system. So capable, in fact, that it serves to this day as a key element of two front-line cruise missiles: the Navy's Tomahawk SLCM and the Air Force's AGM-86B ALCM. TERCOM flight testing began in 1959, under the auspices of the aircraft manufacturer Beech. A succession of flight test programs employing Beech T-29s, assorted Piper types,

The development of practical small jet engines made the highly-compact Tomahawk possible. Of particular significance was the WR-19 turbofan developed by the Williams company for the "flying belt": a one-man, strap-on propulsion pack to convey infantrymen across-country. The WR-19 weighed a paltry 68lb (31kg).

Lockheed C-141 StarLifters, Chance Vought A-7s, Boeing B-52s, drones, and of course cruise missiles themselves, helped coax the system to full maturity.
■ The development of practical small turbojet and turbofan engines. The evolution of such units can be traced back to the Westinghouse turbojet that powered the Navy's Gorgon 2B and 3B air-to-surface missiles in 1945, which was only 9 inches (23cm) in diameter. By 1960, France had developed the Microturbo range of small jet engines, the smallest of which was 12.5 inches (32cm) in diameter and delivered 175lb (780kN) of thrust. In 1962, the American company Williams Research demonstrated its WR-2 turbojet, developing 70lb (310kN) of thrust, which went on to power both the Canadian AN-USD-501 reconnaissance drone and the American MQM-74 target drone.

A great deal of the credit for the leap in cruise missile capabilities must go to the Williams Research Company, which concentrated its efforts on the ultra-small sector of the gas turbine market—indeed, in the United States, it *defined* that market. Of particular significance was the company's proposal, in 1964, to develop a small turbofan engine for the so-called "flying belt": a one-man, strap-on propulsion pack to convey infantrymen across-country at low altitude for up to 10 miles (16km), at speeds of up to 60mph (95kph). The development of such an engine was to have important implications for the future of cruise missiles, because a turbofan is 15 to 20 percent more fuel-efficient at subsonic speeds than a turbojet unit of the same thrust rating, so significant increases in range are attainable. Furthermore, turbofans have smaller acoustical and infrared signatures than turbojets of comparable power output.

The resulting powerplant, the Williams WR-19, emerged in 1967. It developed 430lb (1,910kN) of thrust, weighed a paltry 68lb (31kg), and was one-tenth the size of any other unit capable of that power output. In spite of the inescapable fact that turbofan engines have proportionately larger diameters than comparable turbojet units, the WR-19 measured just 12 inches (30.5cm) in diameter, and was only 24 inches (61cm) in length. Extensive testing at the hands of the US military proved the WR-19 to be both practical and reliable.

Experience gained with Remotely-Piloted Vehicles (RPVs), particularly during the Southeast Asian conflict, helped advance the cruise missile. On reconnaissance missions, the Ryan Firebee functioned with impressive reliability and an uncanny immunity to enemy detection. This Firebee 2 target drone, being recovered during a gunnery meet, gives an idea of this versatile RPV's overall configuration and size.

At around this time, the Air Force, intent on replacing the venerable McDonnell Quail decoy missile, was assessing whether it was feasible to develop an advanced decoy capable of a 2,300-mile (3,200-km) range at a Mach 0.85 cruising speed, and an armed version with the same performance. It proposed that these vehicles—known as the SCUD (Subsonic Cruise Unarmed Decoy) and the SCAM (Subsonic Cruise Attack Missile) respectively—be powered by the WR-19 turbofan described above, or by an engine akin to it. However, the major engine manufacturers were far from confident that such an ambitious performance was attainable with such an engine. In 1968, the Williams company reported that it *would* be possible to achieve such performance if one of the new-generation, high-energy fuels, such as Shelldyne, was employed. In due course, the USAF commissioned Williams to undertake the necessary work.

The SCUD and SCAM programs did not reach fruition, but when the 1970s began, at least the designers of cruise missiles had a small, high-performance turbofan engine available to them in the Williams WR-19.

■ The experience gained with Remotely-Piloted Vehicles (RPVs), particularly during the Southeast Asian conflict. Of especial significance was the success of the Ryan BQM-34A Firebee, an outgrowth of a joint Army/Navy/Air Force program that began with glide tests in March 1951. The Firebee made its maiden flight in December 1958, and found a wide number of uses: primarily reconnaissance missions.

It was in the skies over Southeast Asia that the Firebee achieved distinction. In the process of undertaking more than 3,400 missions, mostly over North Vietnam, it did much to advance the case of RPV advocates—and therefore, indirectly, of cruise missile advocates, too—by functioning with impressive reliability and an uncanny immunity to enemy detection. For firm evidence of the latter quality, one need look no further than the service record of the larger AQM-34L (Model 147SC) variant. Powered by a Teledyne CAE J69-T-41A engine developing 1,920lb (8,540kN) of thrust, this was the most-used Firebee derivative in the Southeast Asian conflict. Of the 1,651 SCs launched, 87.2 percent returned. One, dubbed *Tom Cat*, did not fall prey to enemy defenses until its sixty-ninth sortie, on 25 September 1974.

It should be pointed out that an important factor in these successes was the fact that the Soviet-made radar installations in North Vietnam were not capable of detecting RPVs flying below 300 feet (90m).

■ Work undertaken on a missile known as SCAD (Subsonic Cruise Armed Decoy), which was an outgrowth of the SCUD and SCAM programs to develop a replacement for the Quail decoy missile. None of these advanced decoys was actually flown, but they can be identified collectively as a key step in the evolution of today's cruise missiles. Although the SCAD was primarily conceived as a decoy, there were plans to equip a certain proportion of them with warheads to enhance the system's overall credibility. Guidance was to be achieved with a combination of inertial navigation and TERCOM.

The SCAD was being developed by Boeing, and was to have been powered by the diminutive Williams WR-19 turbofan engine described previously, Williams having beaten Teledyne CAE for the SCAD engine supply contract in April 1973. The SCAD's sizing and configuration was heavily constrained by the Air Force's insistence that it should be installed in the Boeing B-52's existing rotary missile launcher—designed for the Short-Range Attack Missile (SRAM) —the carriage of which had become pivotal to the sizing and configuration of the upcoming Rockwell B-1. Pursuance of this policy not only restricted the SCAD's length and diameter, but also fostered a distinctive trapezoidal fuselage cross-section (to enable more missiles to be accommodated, cake slice-fashion, within the SRAM launcher) and a pronounced "duck bill" nose (to clear the launcher's rotary mechanism).

Unfortunately, the SCAD became something of a political football, and ultimately was canceled—at least in its original form. The Air Force, concerned about undermining the traditional role of the strategic bomber (particularly at a time when the Rockwell B-1 was under development), made strenuous efforts behind the scenes to enhance the SCAD's capabilities as a decoy at the expense of its performance as an armed penetrator: the insistence on compatibility with the SRAM rotary launcher was a good example of this hidden agenda at work. Meanwhile, the Soviet Union was being slow to deploy the defensive systems that could have repulsed an attack by the Air Force's low-flying manned bombers—an AWACS (Airborne Warning and Control System), and MiG-25 *Foxbat* fighter aircraft with a look-down/shoot-down capability—so the SCAD's role was undermined.

Add to this the fact that actual and projected financial outlay on the SCAD program was mushrooming way beyond original estimates and one can appreciate why, in July 1973, the death knell was sounded.

■ The success of Soviet-built cruise missiles in Third World conflicts. This prompted the US Navy to push for the weapon that became the McDonnell Douglas Harpoon antiship missile, which in turn provided a "role model" for the bigger, better US cruise missiles of the future. Like the Air Force, the Navy was predisposed to deride cruise missiles. Its aviators had accomplished many magnificent achievements in World War II, so the service was not about to shift emphasis and jeopardize the future of manned aircraft without good reason.

In October 1967, Soviet-built Styx antiship cruise missiles operated by Egyptian forces inflicted severe damage on the Israeli destroyer *Elath*. This sent shock waves through the military establishment: a reaction not unlike that felt many years later, in 1982, when Argentina used French-built Exocets to devastating effect against British Royal Navy vessels in the Falklands War. McDonnell Douglas had been undertaking studies of antiship missiles since 1965, so when the US Navy —stung by the implications of the *Elath* incident—called for such a weapon, an embryonic program was ripe for development. Initially, the Navy wanted a missile with a range of 45 miles (72km), carrying a 250lb (115kg) conventional warhead. It had to be capable of both air-launching and sea-launching, and it had to be compatible with its existing missile magazines, hoists and launchers (missiles in service with the Navy at that time were the Talos, the Tartar, and the Terrier).

In 1971, McDonnell Douglas won the contract to develop two versions of the missile, one air-launched, the other sea-launched: both dubbed Harpoon. That same year, as if to highlight the potency of cruise missiles, India used the Soviet-built Styx to sink one Pakistani destroyer and badly damage a second. The basic Harpoon made its first flight in December 1972. It could carry a 500lb (230kg) warhead just under 70 miles (110km), and finally entered Navy service in 1977.

■ The miniaturization of nuclear warheads. It goes without saying that the ability to pack so much destructive power into a small envelope helped open the way for smaller, more effective, strategic cruise missiles.

From the melting pot of technologies, experiences and events outlined above, the Tomahawk emerged. But the process was a somewhat tortuous one. For one thing, it was not until 1970 that the concept of a submarine-launched cruise missile received serious consideration. When the Center for Naval Analysis came to the conclusion that such a weapon could indeed be developed, initial discussions centered around the idea of installing a new type of cruise missile in ten of the Navy's aging Polaris-class submarines: three in each of the submarines' sixteen ballistic missile tubes. Other concepts that found favor at that time were a more-capable Harpoon derivative, and an all-new missile dubbed the Submarine Tactical Antiship Weapons System (STAWS).

If there is a point when the Navy's revived interest in cruise missiles can be said to have crystalized, it was in January 1972, when the Secretary of Defense issued an instruction to commence development of a concept known as the Strategic Cruise Missile (SCM). This was renamed the Submarine-Launched Cruise Missile (SLCM) some time later.

In May 1972, the signing of the Strategic Arms Limitation Treaty (SALT) came as an unexpected boost to the cruise missile's prospects. Because the Soviet Union had cruise missiles aplenty, while the Americans had none at that time, it did not press for limitations on them, but concentrated instead on limiting ballistic missiles. Sharp minds in the US military saw the opportunity to actually *increase* their inventory of strategic weapons through the back door.

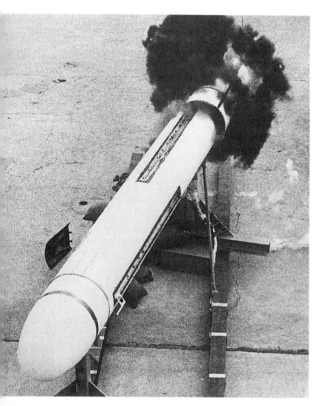

One of a host of distinctive features on the Chance Vought BGM-110 was its "wrap-around" tail fin arrangement, with three curved fins that conformed to the cylindrical shape of the fuselage when stowed. Here, we see the protective shroud being blown clear of the fins and rocket booster motor, allowing the fins to rotate out to the locked position.

During 1972, the quantity and scope of potential Navy cruise missile concepts expanded enormously. As the choice was gradually narrowed down again, STAWS was canceled, and the other concepts were either merged or abandoned, leaving four contenders. In November, the Navy dropped all four and opted instead for a new concept—a SLCM capable of being launched from a torpedo tube. Of course, this decision had important implications for the sizing and configuration of the new missile. Critically, it would restrict it to the length and diameter of the torpedo tube—246 inches (6.25m) and 21 inches (53cm) respectively—and to the lifting capacity of the torpedo handling equipment: 4,200lb (1,910kg).

It was decided that there should be strategic and tactical SLCM variants, but that there should be about 85 percent commonality. Although the Navy stressed the submarine-launching capability, the proposed missile was also to be capable of air and surface launching, and would employ a large measure of existing technology, minimizing development risks. For example, its engine—the Williams F107 turbofan—was a development of the WR-19, the engine that had been selected for the Air Force's aborted SCAD armed decoy missile.

By the summer of 1973, the Air Force's SCAD program was in the throes of cancelation, but was almost immediately reconstituted as the Air-Launched Cruise Missile (ALCM) program when it was realized that this would be a strong bargaining chip in an upcoming round of SALT arms-limitation talks with the Soviets. The Navy and Air Force missiles had much in common, so it made sense when the DoD decreed that summer that the two programs should become the subject of an interservice cooperative effort. The two services, jointly, would develop the key cruise missile technology areas: the Air Force sharing its turbofan engine and high-energy fuel technologies with the Navy, and the Navy sharing its TERCOM guidance system technology with the Air Force. It was proposed that deployment of the ALCM should take place in late 1978, while the SLCM should be deployed some time in 1980.

(The initials SLCM, which originally had stood for *Submarine*-Launched Cruise Missile, in time came to stand for *Sea*-Launched Cruise Missile, to account for the fact that the missile was intended for launching by surface vessels, too).

In December 1973, the Pentagon instructed the Navy to organize a competitive flyoff to select its SLCM contractor. The following month, the two closest contenders were separated out from the other applicants: the BGM-109, proposed by the Convair Division of General Dynamics, with Williams as the engine supplier and McDonnell Douglas as the guidance system supplier; and the BGM-110, proposed by Chance Vought (by now part of the LTV corporation), with Teledyne CAE as the engine supplier and E-Systems as the guidance system supplier. By September 1975, at least one thing had been decided. Whoever won the flyoff, the winning design would be named for the fighting axe used by the North American Indians—the Tomahawk.

A lesser, though vital, flyoff competition was held to select the common guidance system. E-Systems, originator of the TERCOM system, was roundly beaten by McDonnell Douglas, which employed off-the-shelf components in its system. This situation came about because E-Systems had only patented one particular form of TERCOM system. The US government held the rights to most of the developmental work that had gone into the TERCOM principle, so it was perfectly in order for McDonnell

Douglas to devise its own version. An Air Force C-141 was employed for the tests. It flew an identical series of 1,300-mile (2,080-km) courses for both of the competing systems. The guidance system contract was awarded in October 1975.

The "battle proper" was fought out in early 1976. The designs that Convair/ General Dynamics and Vought fielded to meet the Navy's stringent requirements

Another novel feature of the Chance Vought BGM-110 was its one-piece fiber glass wing, which was stowed longitudinally within the fuselage and swung through 90 degrees about a shoulder-mounted pivot, protruding through protected slots high on the fuselage sides, as seen here.

—which included a range in the bracket 1,500-1,600 miles (2,400-2,560km)—differed markedly.

Convair/General Dynamics' BGM-109 was powered by a Williams F107-WR-100 turbofan, had a solid-propellant rocket booster motor to provide the first few seconds of thrust, and had a welded aluminium fuselage measuring 18 feet (5.5m) in length and 1.8 feet (0.55m) in diameter. Its aluminium wings were stowed within the fuselage on a scissor-like mechanism, one above the other. Thus, when the wings were deployed—through protected slots in the fuselage sides—one wing was higher than the other. The BGM-109's wingspan measured 8.5 feet (2.6m). The tail fins were also stowed within the fuselage, but on more conventional "pop-out" mechanisms. Four tail fins deployed in a cruciform (+-shaped) arrangement.

Ranged against this clean and thoroughly functional design was the more radical Chance Vought contender, the BGM-110. Powered by a Teledyne CAE 471-11DX turbofan, it had a stainless steel fuselage measuring 17.8 feet (5.4m) in length, with the solid rocket booster adding a further 32 inches (1m). One of a host of distinctive features was its one-piece fiber glass wing, which was stowed longitudinally within the fuselage and swung through 90 degrees about a shoulder-mounted pivot, protruding through protected slots high on the fuselage sides. Its wingspan measured 10.5 feet (3.2m).

Another novel feature of the Vought design was its "wrap-around" tail fin arrangement, with three curved fins that conformed to the cylindrical shape of the fuselage when stowed. Thus, the fins were stowed externally, rather than recessed within the fuselage, and on deployment they simply rotated on their hinges to reach the locked position.

The flyoff did not go well for Vought's innovative missile, however. The competitors were each to be given two attempts to perform at least one successful transition from an underwater launch, through the boost phase, and into gliding flight. The Convair/General Dynamics BGM-109 went first and achieved a 100 percent success record by making two flawless transitions, on 13 and 15 February 1976. Vought's first attempt was declared void, due to a torpedo tube malfunction (the Navy accepted sole responsibility for this fault). On its second attempt, the BGM-110 demonstrated that it had the ability to transition from water to air, but then its one-piece wing failed to deploy. A further test was scheduled for 24 March, but on 8 March the Navy pulled the plug on Vought's efforts. Its decision was influenced not only by the recalcitrance of the BGM-110's wing mechanism, but also by cost overruns, and by the BGM-109's two excellent performances.

On 17 March, General Dynamics was awarded a contract to supply the Navy with BGM-109 Tomahawk SLCMs, and in May the Williams company was awarded a contract to supply the engines for them. Another key event took place on 28 March, when the Tomahawk SLCM made its first free flight, air-launched from an Air Force Boeing B-52.

Throughout the period 1973-1977, the Navy's Tomahawk SLCM program and the Air Force's ALCM program continued to converge. Commonality was to be achieved wherever practicable—the two missiles certainly would share a common warhead, guidance system and turbofan engine—and there were efforts to get the two programs to achieve common developmental milestones. The key contractors in the ALCM program remained those which had developed the SCAD. Boeing was still in charge of development, and Williams still served as the engine contractor, supplying the WR-19-derived F107 turbofan. The Boeing AGM-86A, to give the ALCM its proper designation, was to retain the key features of the SCAD: the trapezoidal fuselage cross-section, the distinctive "duck bill" nose, the engine air intake mounted just forward of the vertical stabilizer, the fold-up anhedral tail fins, and the slender dihedral wings—stowed switch blade fashion beneath the fuselage for launch, swept back 35 degrees when extended to their full 115-inch (2.9-m) span.

A nuclear warhead would replace the SCAD's electronic countermeasures (ECM) package, twenty-one ECM antennas were to be deleted, metal would replace fiber glass in the wing construction, and elevons were to replace the elevators and ailerons. At a cruising speed of Mach 0.65-0.85, the missile would fly up to 750 miles (1,200km).

The first jettison test of an AGM-86A ALCM from a SRAM rotary launcher took place in June 1975, and the missile's first powered flight took place on 5 March 1976. Dropped from the weapons bay of a B-52 at 10,000 feet (3,050m), the AGM-86A flew for about 10 minutes, reaching a maximum speed of Mach 0.65. On 9 September, on its fourth powered flight, the AGM-86A demonstrated that it could navigate successfully. Although it crashed just short of its target—due to an insufficient quantity of fuel being placed aboard—it employed TERCOM four times, and flew as low as 30 feet (10m) off the undulating terrain during its 31-minute flight.

AGM-86A test missiles were not fitted with recovery systems, so they could not be reused. Consequently, flight testing of the ALCM progressed at a slower rate than that of the Tomahawk

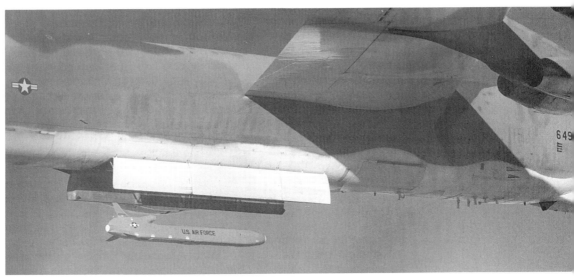

A Boeing AGM-86B is dropped from the bomb bay of a B-52 during the competitive flyoff with the AGM-109 Tomahawk that decided which missile would become the Air Force's Air-Launched Cruise Missile (ALCM). The Boeing missile, which was optimized from the outset for the air-launched mission, won the contest.

43

SLCM. Test Tomahawks, equipped with parachutes and flotation gear, could be rapidly recycled: about 80 percent of them were reflown. Furthermore, the Tomahawk suffered fewer flight test failures. For these reasons, the Navy steadily clawed away at the Air Force's original two-year developmental lead, to catch and then beat the ALCM to key milestones. For example, the Tomahawk SLCM made its first fully guided test flight, lasting 61 minutes, in June 1976—three months ahead of the AGM-86A ALCM's first fully guided flight. During the course of 1976, the Tomahawk SLCM flew sixteen times, amassing about 13 hours of flying time. In the same period, the AGM-86A ALCM flew only six times, spending little more than 1 hour aloft.

The relatively slow pace of the ALCM program stemmed from the Air Force's deep-seated belief that cruise missiles were inferior to manned penetrating bombers. It ranked the ALCM third in its order of priorities, well behind its new manned bomber, the Rockwell B-1, and its new intercontinental ballistic missile (ICBM), the MX. However, the Air Force viewpoint was becoming increasingly out of step with the changing political climate. The Navy's progress with the Tomahawk SLCM only served to highlight the Air Force's footdragging with the ALCM, which had not gone unnoticed on Capitol Hill. In late 1975, the House of Representatives temporarily suspended funding for the ALCM. Then, overestimating the similarity between the ALCM and the Tomahawk, Congress considered employing the latter to do the former's role, estimating a cost saving of around $300 million in early 1977. It became clear that if the Air Force brass did not take proper steps to develop a viable cruise missile for themselves, the Navy would be asked to do it for them.

An understandable reluctance to have this happen caused the Air Force to pursue the ALCM program with renewed vigor. An even greater injection of impetus followed President Jimmy Carter's sudden cancelation of the Rockwell B-1 bomber on 30 June 1977, because the Air Force would now have to rely on a cruise missile to form the air-breathing leg of its nuclear Triad (the other two elements being land-based ballistic missiles and ballistic missile-equipped submarines).

To ensure that the Air Force got the best missile for the ALCM role, the DoD ordered a competitive flyoff between the AGM-86 and an air-launched derivative of the Tomahawk SLCM, designated AGM-109, but also known as the Tomahawk Air-Launched Cruise Missile (TALCM). The main difference between the sea-launched Tomahawk and its air-launched derivative was the deletion of the former's rocket booster motor. Both missiles would be launched from a B-52 (in earlier test flights, the Tomahawk had been launched from a Grumman A-6 Intruder), and the flyoff was to comprize: "captive-carry" sorties, in which the missile remained mated to the B-52 to assess the aerodynamic and structural characteristics of the missile/parent aircraft combination, and the efficacy of the mechanical and electronic links between them and data-gathering (via telemetry) equipment on the ground; "drop-test" sorties, in which the missile would be released from the B-52 in flight, but the engine left inert; and, finally, a series of competitive ALCM sorties.

In order to increase the AGM-86's range, Boeing "stretched" the fuselage, providing greater fuel capacity. At 1,500 miles (2,400km), its range was now comparable to that of the Tomahawk. However, in its elongated form—designated AGM-86B—the new variant would not fit the B-52's SRAM rotary launcher (while the Tomahawk was never intended to do so). This and other complications caused the flyoff to be rescheduled and postponed several times.

The Tomahawk ALCM's first free flight took place on 17 July 1979. The first ten flights yielded four crashes, but 22.2 hours of free-flying time was amassed. The missile's final flight took place on 8 February 1980. The AGM-86B's maiden flight took place on 3 August 1979. The Boeing missile also undertook ten flights. As with the Tomahawk ALCM, four ended in crashes. The AGM-86B notched up 31.7 hours in free flight: almost one-third more than the General Dynamics missile. An evaluation board comprizing over 200 Air Force and Navy officers came to a unanimous decision. The Secretary of the Air Force, Hans Mark, announced that the AGM-86B had won the flyoff, citing its superior terrain-following capabilities and forecasting an easier, cheaper maintenance regime. The USAF awarded a contract for 3,418 ALCMs to Boeing in March 1980. Test-flying of the AGM-86B continued after the flyoff, and the missile went on to achieve full operational status in December 1982, equipping SAC B-52Gs and B-52Hs. The air-launched Tomahawk variant was terminated.

Superiority of the AGM-86B over the AGM-109 in Air Force terms can be attributed to the fact that Boeing's missile had been optimized from the outset for the air-launched mission. The AGM-86B is, in effect, a scaled-down aircraft, whereas the Tomahawk is a winged torpedo. Although the Tomahawk lost this particular contest, it went on to carve a reputation for itself in Navy and, later, Army hands—in sea-launched and ground-launched forms respectively— that has eclipsed that of its erstwhile rival.

On 19 March 1980, the first Tomahawk firing from a surface vessel, the destroyer USS *Merrill* (DD-976), took place. After successfully completing pre-service trials, the Tomahawk became operational with the Navy a few months after the ALCM entered Air Force service, being distributed for installation in a wide variety of vessels. Just as the ALCM had breathed new life into the venerable B-52, so the introduction of the Tomahawk SLCM resurrected the Navy's mighty Iowa-class (BB) battleships: *New Jersey, Missouri, Wisconsin,* and *Iowa.* These four leviathans had been held in storage as part of the Navy's Inactive Fleet, cared for by a skeleton crew. The first to undergo refurbishment and modernization, at a cost of $326 million, was the USS *New Jersey*—the "Big Jay"— the task being completed in December 1982.

After only a few years of service, the Iowa-class vessels began to be progressively withdrawn, on the grounds that they were too costly to operate. However, two of them stayed in service long enough to see action in the Gulf War. The Iowa-class ships (displacement, 45,000 tons) were capable of carrying up to thirty-two Tomahawks.

Today, vessels capable of carrying the Tomahawk include the Ticoneroga-class (CG) cruisers and the Spruance-class (DD) destroyers. Tomahawks are also carried aboard a large number of submarines, including the Sturgeon-class (SSN) and the Los Angeles-class (SSN) vessels. The Sturgeon-class submarines can only launch Tomahawks through their torpedo tubes, whereas some of the Los Angeles-class submarines are also equipped to launch the missiles vertically.

Having traced the Tomahawk's origins, we can now examine the missile's anatomy in greater depth.

Chapter 3

Anatomy of the Tomahawk

A Modular Weapon System

Tomahawks are modular in construction. The assorted variants differ in respect to their warheads, fuel tank configurations, and guidance systems, but share a common airframe/engine design. Broadly speaking, all Tomahawks are identical from the wings back.

The foremost module is the guidance section, a fiber glass-and-aluminium nose fairing that houses the guidance system. The antiship variant's guidance system is distinctly different from that installed aboard the land-attack Tomahawks, and is therefore dealt with separately in the appropriate chapter. Guidance systems for the land-attack Tomahawks are manufactured by Litton Guidance and Control at its Salt Lake City, Utah, facility, with research and development being undertaken at its Woodland Hills, California, facility. There are two primary elements to the system: an inertial guidance set and a digital computer. These are collectively referred to as the Reference Measuring Unit Computer (RMUC).

Throughout this book, the term "guidance system," where it applies to land-attack Tomahawks, can be taken to encompass the RMUC, with the TERCOM terrain-matching facility resident in the computer's memory, a radar altimeter, and, in the case of the C and D variants, a terminal guidance system known as the Digital Scene-Matching Area Correlator (DSMAC), plus some associated hardware. Cruise Missile Guidance Set (CMGS) is the acronym applied to the full ensemble.

Behind the guidance section is either a one- or two-element portion known variously as the forward body payload section/forward body section (A and G variants), the forward body payload section (B variant), the fuel tank/forward body payload section (C variant), and the payload section/fuel tank (D variant). The profusion of titles results from the fact that the internal configuration of this portion of the missile varies from one variant to another. On the nuclear-tipped A and G variants, due to the comparatively small warhead size, it constitutes a significant forward extension of the main fuel-carrying area. On the B variant it constitutes an aft extension of the area available to the guidance system, and houses a conventional 1,000lb (454kg) warhead. On the C variant it houses some fuel and the same conventional warhead that the B variant carries, while on the D variant it houses a submunitions dispenser and a small quantity of fuel.

Directly aft of that is the mid-body section, a structure that serves as the main fuel-carrying area and as a housing for the wings, which are stowed one atop the other. Behind this is the aft-body section, the upper portion of which serves as the aft extremity of the fuel tank. The lower portion houses an extendable air intake for the cruise-phase powerplant.

Behind the aft-body section is the propulsion section. This houses the cruise-phase powerplant: a Williams International F107-WR-400 low-bypass turbofan developing 600lb (2,670kN) of thrust. Williams manufactures this engine at its Ogden, Utah, facility. The propulsion section has a near-cylindrical exterior, to conform to the missile's overall shape. Its inner structure, however, tapers to form a truncated cone that serves as the mounting point for the boost-phase powerplant. The propulsion section also houses four pneumatic-ally-deployed tail fins, which steer the Tomahawk in response to commands from the guidance system.

At the extreme rear of the Tomahawk is the boost-phase powerplant: a Type 106 solid-propellant rocket motor manufactured by dual-source suppliers Atlantic Research Corporation (ARC), of Gainesville, Virginia, and United Technologies Chemical Systems Division, of

Tomahawks undergoing final assembly. The assorted variants differ in respect to their warheads, fuel tank configurations, and guidance systems, but share a common airframe/engine design. Broadly speaking, all Tomahawks are identical from the wings back.

San Jose, California. The solid rocket motor develops 6,000lb (26,690kN) of thrust for a period of 12 seconds, propelling the missile clear of its parent vessel, after which it is jettisoned.

For transport, handling and loading, the Tomahawk stays encapsulated in a stainless steel capsule (this is also known as a canister: the name varies according to the nature of the launch system). When firing takes place, this canister conveys the missile along the launching tube, but is retained within the tube. As one might expect, underwater launches are a more complex affair than those made directly into the air from launch platforms mounted on the decks of surface vessels because the missile's internal pressure must be brought into alignment with the ambient pressure when the launching tube is flooded. A

hydraulic device propels the missile along the tube, and the retained capsule is subsequently ejected. When the missile is 30ft (9m) from the submarine, a lanyard ignites the booster motor, propelling the missile to the surface. It broaches the surface at a speed of about 75fps (23mps). When it is clear of the water, various protective covers are jettisoned.

From this point on, the underwater and surface launching sequences are identical. The four tail fins deploy and guide the missile through a 180-degree roll. With this maneuver completed, the wings are deployed by means of a pyrotechnic device and lock in place. Doors in the missile's flanks open to let the wings swing out, then close again to streamline the slots through which the wings protrude. At the culmination of the launch sequence, the underbelly air

The Tomahawk is modular in construction. The foremost module is the guidance section, *a fiber glass-and-aluminium nose fairing that houses the guidance system.*

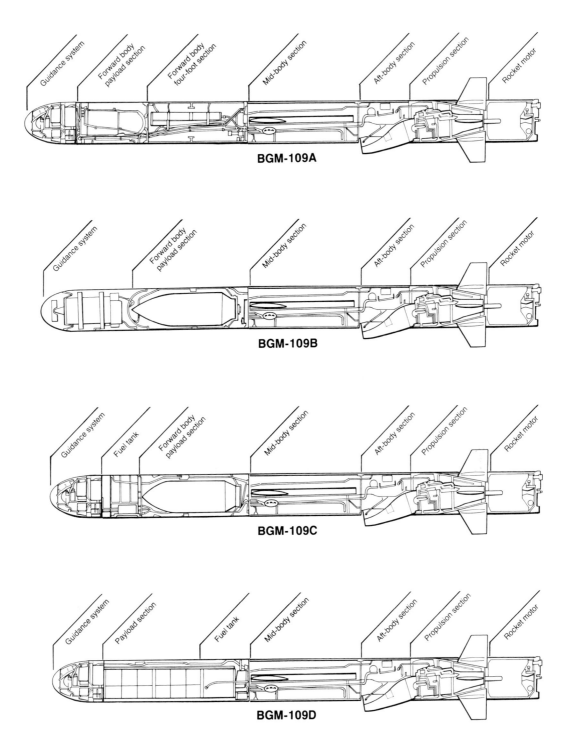

BGM-109A

BGM-109B

BGM-109C

BGM-109D

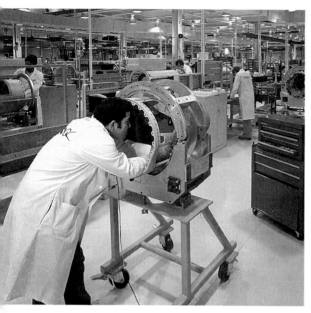

Tomahawk tail cones in their assembly jigs.

This diminutive powerplant is one of the keys to the Tomahawk's success. It is a Williams International F107-WR-400 low-bypass turbofan developing 600lb (2,670kN) of thrust. Williams manufactures this engine at its Ogden, Utah, facility.

intake extends, the spent boost-phase motor is jettisoned, and a gas cartridge fires to start the cruise-phase engine.

Today, McDonnell Douglas Aerospace-East and Hughes Missile Systems Company both produce Tomahawks under an annual competitive procurement program (Hughes acquired the missile programs of General Dynamics Convair Division in 1992). In addition, the two companies compete for their respective shares of depot maintenance and remanufacturing work each year. Final assembly of Tomahawks takes place at McDonnell Douglas Aerospace-East's facility at Titusville, Florida, just a few miles from NASA's Kennedy Space Center, and Hughes Missile Systems Company's facility at Tucson, Arizona. Components are shipped to these sites by subcontractors across the United States.

General Dynamics Convair Division delivered its 1,000th Tomahawk to the US Navy in May 1989. Another significant landmark was passed in July 1991, when McDonnell Douglas delivered its 1,000th Tomahawk. To date, no Tomahawks have been sold abroad.

While researching this book, the author paid a visit to McDonnell Douglas Aerospace-East's dedicated Tomahawk production facility at Titusville. The corporation invested over $100 million in buildings and equipment at this site, which was completed in 1982. Tomahawk production started there in October of the following year. With its computer-driven work stations, modern computer-controlled machine tools and test equipment, and a fully-automated inventory management system, the Titusville plant is highly impressive. Seven hundred personnel are employed at Titusville. A further 200 personnel are assigned to Tomahawk-related work at the corporation's St. Louis, Missouri, facility.

There are four elements to the Tomahawk Weapon System (TWS). Listed in the order required to execute a mission, they are: the Tomahawk Mission Planning Center (TMPC), a manned, computerized facility in which the flight path is painstakingly planned, the risks assessed, the software necessary to undertake the mission written, and the mission simulated; the Tomahawk Weapon Control System (TWCS) platform, the shipboard fire-control system that takes the software required to perform a mission, which is held on a disk, and prepares it for loading into the missile; the Launching System, which may take the form of an armored box launcher, a submarine torpedo tube, a

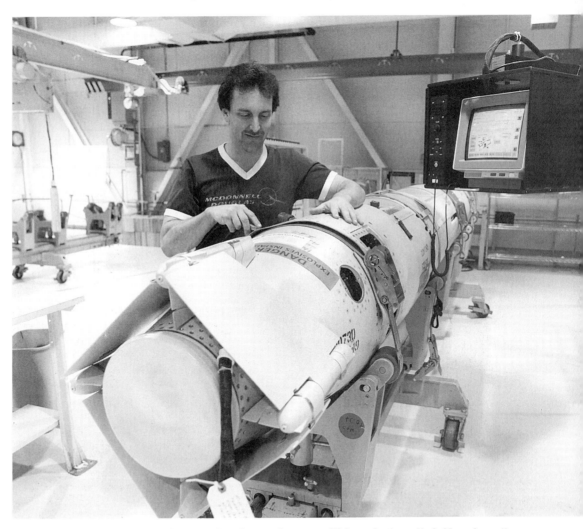

This view of the aft end of the Tomahawk reveals the point where the solid rocket booster will later be installed. Note the tail fin folding arrangement.

submarine capsule launching system, or a surface vessel vertical launching system; and the All-Up Round, which is the official name for the missile itself.

Tomahawks are usually placed aboard vessels in a mix of variants. For example, there might be a combination of B, C and D variants aboard a particular vessel at a given time. Details as to the total quantity of missiles actually being carried, and the combination of variants, are not revealed.

The designations of the assorted Tomahawk variants can be confusing to the uninitiated. Under the original nomenclature, Tomahawks were designated

BGM-109, the *B* denoting *boosted*, the *G* denoting *guided*, and the *M* denoting *missile*. To differentiate between surface-launched and submarine-launched Tomahawks, the suffix 1 denoted the former, and the suffix 2 denoted the latter. The Navy applied a new system of nomenclature to the Tomahawk in the mid-1980s, in which the distinction between surface-launched and submarine-launched missiles was made by means of a prefix, the *B* being supplanted by either *R* (denoting surface-launched), or *U* (denoting underwater-launched). Thus, the surface-launched version of the C-variant Tomahawk, which had

Tomahawks can be launched from armored box launchers (pictured), submarine torpedo *tubes, submarine capsule launching systems, or surface vessel vertical launching systems.*

previously been designated BGM-109C1, was henceforth designated RGM-109C.

A parallel nomenclature operates within the Tomahawk program: one that puts phases of the missile's development into a chronological context, differentiating between one developmental phase (Block) and another. Thus, over the years, there have been Block 1, Block 1A, Block 2, Block 2A, Block 2B, and Block 3 missiles, and soon there will be Block 4 missiles.

Tomahawks are test-flown periodically, to maintain proficiency and/or assess new developments. In the case of the land-attack Tomahawk variants, this inevitably involves overland flights. At the time of writing, Tomahawks launched from surface vessels and submarines have conducted overflights of Alabama, Alaska, California, Florida, Maine, Nevada, and Utah. These flights have, on occasion, drawn opposition from peace campaigners and other concerned parties. In 1989, Tomahawk flights over Maine prompted a non-binding referendum to poll public opinion. Objectors won the vote by a narrow margin— although the turnout was poor, with less than one-third of registered voters participating. The Navy acknowledged the concerns of the protesters, but the overflights continued.

Unlike operational Tomahawks, or those being test-flown with a live warhead, Tomahawks assigned to non-destructive flight tests incorporate special hardware. In place of the warhead, a system known as the Recovery Exercise Module (REM) can be carried. This allows a test engineer in an accompanying chase aircraft to remotely-control the Tomahawk if that proves necessary and either bring it safely to earth with a built-in parachute recovery system, or cause the missile to perform a destructive dive into the ocean if it is likely to threaten life or property. Alternatively, a device known as the Range Safety System (RSS) can be carried. This performs a similar function to the REM, but does not incorporate a parachute recovery system, so the mission can only be terminated with a destructive dive into the ocean.

Both the REM and the RSS incorporate a telemetry package to relay data on critical performance parameters to the chase aircraft and/or the ground control center, or even to a high-flying support aircraft (the Navy's flight test center at Patuxent River, Maryland has a specially-equipped Convair 880 that can collect telemetered data, and also relay it to the ground control center, providing welcome redundancy).

In 1989, General Dynamics Convair Division was awarded a Cruise Missiles Project Office contract worth $27 million to update the REM and RSS, by consolidating several components and simplifying installation.

For test flights in which a live warhead is carried, the REM and RSS are not required. Typically, a test flight of this type might start with a Tomahawk being launched vertically from a permanent pad facility on San Nicholas Island in the Pacific Missile Test Center range, off Southern California. At the culmination of such a test, the Tomahawk might strike a steel-and-concrete bunker on San Clemente Island, some 50 miles (80km) off Los Angeles. The warehouse-sized target typically would be composed of concrete slabs, individually numbered to aid photographic analysis. The slabs, each weighing 7,000lb (3,180kg), are thrown high into the air by the blast.

Having outlined the basic elements of the TWS, the next few chapters examine the individual Tomahawk variants in greater depth.

Chapter 4

Nuclear-Tipped Tomahawks

The A and G Variants

Since the Tomahawk was principally conceived as a strategic nuclear weapon, we will examine the nuclear-tipped variants first. There have been two—the A and G variants—but neither are deployed today. The A-variant missile was the first nuclear warhead-toting Tomahawk variant, and remains a potent "sleeping" element in the US Navy's armory. Following an undertaking made by President George Bush in early 1991, it was withdrawn from service and placed in what is termed "ready storage" at naval weapons stations. However, the missiles can still be rapidly redeployed if that is deemed necessary at some point in the future.

The A-variant Tomahawk can carry a weapon with many times the destructive power of the bombs dropped on Hiroshima and Nagasaki up to 1,500 miles (2,400km). It is by far the most capable Tomahawk in terms of range. It navigates to its target by means of a Litton inertial guidance set, a Honeywell radar altimeter, and TERCOM (Terrain Contour Matching): a software subsystem that functions within the onboard Litton digital computer. The missile is officially titled the Nuclear Land-Attack Tomahawk, or TLAM-N (Tomahawk Land Attack Missile-N for Nuclear). Its warhead, designated W-80, is encased in a cylindrical structure, the precise nature of which is highly classified.

When the A-variant missile entered US Navy service in 1984, it became the second Tomahawk SLCM variant to achieve operational status. The final order for A-variant Tomahawks was placed in 1990, and the last missile was delivered in 1992 (it normally takes eighteen months to two years to manufacture a Tomahawk and undertake the necessary pre-delivery tests). The A variant is the lightest member of the Tomahawk family. At the moment of emergence from the launcher, less capsule, but complete with booster, warhead, and a full fuel load, the surface-launched version of the A-variant missile—originally known as the BGM-109A1 but since redesignated RGM-109A—weighs 3,180lb (1,445kg). The submarine-launched version—originally known as the BGM-109A2 but since redesignated UGM-109A—weighs 3,260lb (1,480kg): about 80lb (36kg) more, due to the additional weight of various waterproof protective covers and a pressure venting device that allows the missile to equalize its internal and external air pressures as it rises through the water.

It is not possible to list which vessels actually carried the A variant when it was deployed, because the Navy has a policy of neither confirming nor denying that specific vessels are, or are not, carrying nuclear weapons at any given time. What it *will* confirm is that *all* surface combatants—namely cruisers, destroyers, and (until their recent withdrawal from service) battleships, as well as attack submarines—were, and are, equally capable of fielding the nuclear-tipped Tomahawk.

Assuming the nuclear option was to be exercised, and the A-variant Tomahawk redeployed as a consequence, this is what a typical mission would entail.

Once launched from its parent ship —be it a surface vessel or a submarine— the missile would jettison the various covers, extend its tail fins, wings and engine air intake, complete the boost phase by jettisoning its solid rocket booster, then activate the turbofan engine to transition to the cruise phase, establishing a speed of Mach 0.5–0.75 for the journey to its target. Its inertial guidance system would be the sole means by which it navigated its passage over the sea.

The missile would undertake the

The A-variant Tomahawk can carry a weapon with many times the destructive power of the bombs dropped on Hiroshima and Nagasaki up to 1,500 miles (2,400km). Following an undertaking made by President George Bush in early 1991, it was withdrawn from service and placed in what is termed "ready storage" at naval weapons stations. It can still be rapidly redeployed if that is deemed necessary.

cruise phase in either a "high-low" altitude regime for optimum range, or a "low-low" regime for optimum immunity from enemy detection. The latter regime has a fuel-consumption penalty because the air is more dense at lower altitudes, causing the missile to incur higher aerodynamic drag factors. However, the A-variant Tomahawk is well equipped to counter such conditions, because its nuclear warhead, being smaller and lighter than the conventional warheads carried by other Tomahawk variants, permits a much greater fuel load to be carried. This is the key to the A-variant's impressive range.

Regardless of whether it flew a high-low regime or a low-low regime in the cruise phase, the missile would cross the coastline of the first land mass at low altitude. Its radar altimeter would be switched on just before the missile made this important transition from over-water to over-land flight (important, because it cues a new mode of navigation), and would proceed to relay altitude data to the onboard computer for the remainder of the mission.

The Tomahawk's flight over land is a constant compromise between flying too high, thereby risking detection by enemy radars and the attendant possibility of being downed by enemy ground defenses, and flying too low, thereby

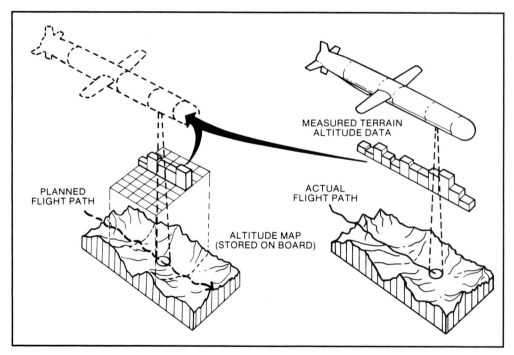

PLANNED
FLIGHT PATH

MEASURED TERRAIN
ALTITUDE DATA

ACTUAL
FLIGHT PATH

ALTITUDE MAP
(STORED ON BOARD)

Terrain Contour Matching (TERCOM) allows the Tomahawk to refine the accuracy of its flight path by comparing a series of terrain elevation profiles gathered by the radar altimeter with digital ground contour maps of corresponding geographical areas stored in the computer memory. These comparisons update the inertial guidance system and indicate how much adjustment should be made to the flight path to maintain the correct course.

risking a crash (the Tomahawk program people call it a "ground clobber"). Mission planners resolve this compromise to the best of their ability prior to flight, drawing upon all the information at their disposal, then a disk bearing all of the necessary instructions is loaded into the Tomahawk's computer. From the moment of launch, the Tomahawk flies totally autonomously, functioning entirely in accordance with the instructions loaded into its computer beforehand.

Aside from its small size, and its ability to fly an evasive course at high subsonic speeds and extremely low altitudes—typically, below 100ft (30m) —a major contributor to the Tomahawk's survivability is the fact that its radar altimeter always looks directly down, not forward. A forward-looking system,

as fitted to the B-52 and FB-111, would allow the missile to fly even lower, but radiating a signal forward would greatly increase the risk of enemy detection. As it is, an enemy jamming device would need to be sited virtually directly beneath the speeding Tomahawk to disable it, and to achieve that in anything other than purely coincidental circumstances, the enemy would have to know the missile's route in advance.

With a downward-looking system, there is the burning question about what happens when the missile approaches a prominent vertical obstacle, such as a sheer cliff face! The answer is that mission planners must program the missile to alter its altitude in sufficient time to clear the obstacle in question.

TERCOM allows the Tomahawk to

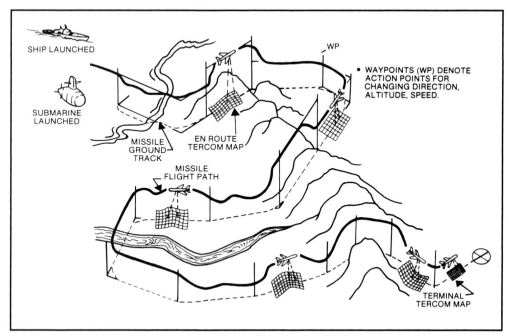

This diagram shows in a simplified manner how the Tomahawk navigates its way over land by undertaking a series of TERCOM fixes. In actual fact, a series of groupings of

TERCOM maps are required for a mission. These are known collectively as a map set. The distance between TERCOM maps is a closely-guarded secret.

refine the accuracy of its flight path by comparing a series of terrain elevation profiles gathered by the radar altimeter with digital ground contour maps of corresponding geographical areas stored in the computer memory. These comparisons update the inertial guidance system and indicate how much adjustment should be made to the flight path to maintain the correct course. The geographical areas—which are rectangular in shape and are referred to as maps—lie at pre-selected points (waypoints) along the route where a specific action must take place: it may be a point where a change in direction is required, or a change in altitude or speed, or it may be a point where the Tomahawk's radar altimeter must begin scanning the

ground, or it may simply be a point where the missile must confirm its position and altitude. The TERCOM maps become progressively smaller as the target is approached, so that the Tomahawk is directed with ever-increasing precision.

A series of groupings of TERCOM maps are required for a mission. These are known collectively as a map set. The distance between TERCOM maps is a closely-guarded secret. TERCOM maps are selected by mission planners prior to launch, employing data supplied by the Defense Mapping Agency (DMA) and other intelligence sources, including data from reconnaissance satellites. TERCOM does not tend to be affected by snow covering, because a uniform layer of snow, conforming to the terrain features,

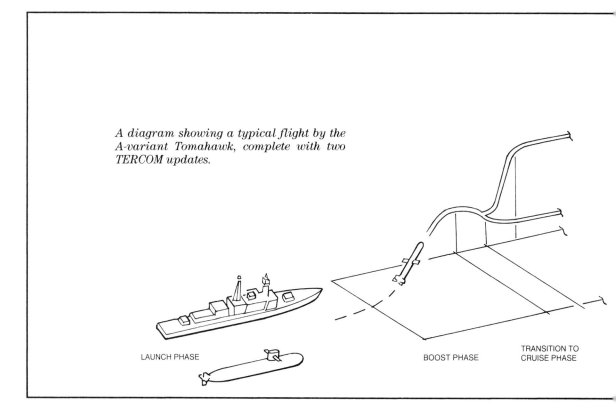

A diagram showing a typical flight by the A-variant Tomahawk, complete with two TERCOM updates.

LAUNCH PHASE

BOOST PHASE

TRANSITION TO
CRUISE PHASE

cannot help but maintain their relative heights. At the opposite extreme, when flying over desert areas, sand dunes are of no use to TERCOM, because their height and shape alter at the mercy of the wind.

The combination of inertial guidance, the radar altimeter and TERCOM would get the A-variant Tomahawk to within several hundred feet of the aim point. This is sufficiently accurate for the delivery of a nuclear weapon. Land-attack Tomahawks with conventional warheads carry a second navigation-updating system, the Digital Scene-Matching Area Correlator (DSMAC), to provide truly pinpoint targeting precision, but with a nuclear warhead, which has a large destructive footprint, there is no

need for such a high-accuracy system. The A variant's warhead would be detonated directly above the target. If necessary, in the final seconds of flight, the missile would either climb or dive to reach the optimum altitude for detonation.

Following a recommendation by the Defense Systems Acquisition Review Council (DSARC) in January 1977, a ground-launched Tomahawk was developed from the sea-launched A variant, to serve as a mobile theater nuclear weapon. This new Tomahawk was officially known as the Ground-Launched Cruise Missile (GLCM), and was appropriately designated BGM-109G. It was operated by the US Air Force, and had about 90 percent commonality with the

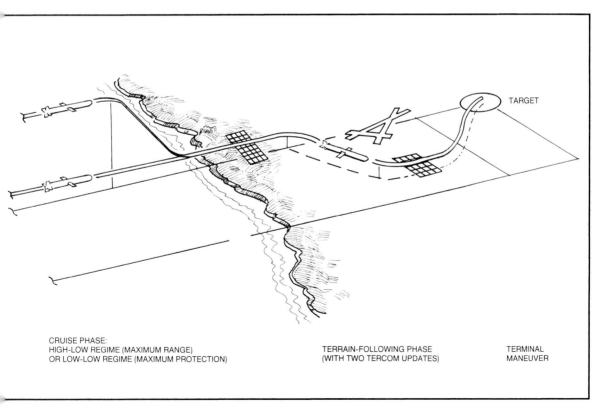

CRUISE PHASE:
HIGH-LOW REGIME (MAXIMUM RANGE)
OR LOW-LOW REGIME (MAXIMUM PROTECTION)

TERRAIN-FOLLOWING PHASE
(WITH TWO TERCOM UPDATES)

TERMINAL
MANEUVER

Following a recommendation by the Defense Systems Acquisition Review Council (DSARC) in 1977, a ground-launched Tomahawk was development from the sea-launched A variant. Known officially as the Ground Launched Cruise Missile (GLCM) and designated BGM-109G, it was operated by the US Air Force in Western Europe, but has since been withdrawn. Here, a GLCM streaks from its Transporter-Erector-Launcher (TEL).

A-variant SLCM operated by the Navy.

Like the A variant, the GLCM had a range of 1,500 miles (2,400km). The primary differences between the A and G variants were the warhead (the G variant toted a W-84 device, which differed from the A variant's W-80, but no-one will say precisely *how* it differed), and the G variant's even more extensive built-in self-test (BIT) capability. BIT both assesses the missile's general airworthiness and verifies the health of its systems. With the A variant Tomahawk, BIT was a vital facet of pre-launch preparations, not only to ensure the safety of the parent ship, but also to ensure that the missile would reach its destination before the warhead detonated. With the G-variant Tomahawk, a precautionary BIT sequence was run once a month, irrespective of whether a launch was to take place or not.

At the moment of emergence from the launcher, less canister, but complete with booster, warhead, and a full fuel load, the Tomahawk GLCM weighed 3,250lb (1,475kg)—about 70lb (32kg) more than the A-variant Tomahawk: the differential probably arose from a difference in warhead weight, but this has never been officially confirmed.

The G-variant Tomahawk was launched from a huge multi-wheeled vehicle known as a Transporter-Erector-Launcher (TEL). This featured an upward-pivoting armored box that carried four missiles. TELs were complemented by mobile Launch Control Centers (LCCs). In terms of command structure, it was decided that Tomahawk GLCMs should be organized into flights of four TELs, and that each flight should be assigned two LCCs: a primary and a backup. With the obvious exception of the over-water phase, the GLCM navigated to its target in precisely the same manner as the A-variant Tomahawk, employing an inertial guidance set and a radar altimeter to make its way from one grouping of TERCOM maps to the next.

In December 1979, NATO accepted an American proposal that a force of nuclear-tipped theater missiles, comprising 464 US Air Force Tomahawk GLCMs and 108 US Army Pershing 2 ballistic missiles, be based in Western Europe as part of the United States' contribution to that organization. Under that proposal, the United Kingdom was to house 160 Tomahawk GLCMs, Italy 112, West Germany ninety-six, and Belgium and Holland forty-eight apiece.

Flight testing of Tomahawk GLCMs took place at Dugway Proving Grounds, Utah, under the auspices of the Air Force Tactical Air Warfare Center. On 16 May 1980, the Tomahawk GLCM made its first flight, launched from a TEL missile tube mounted on a concrete pad. In February 1981, the Tomahawk GLCM made its first launch from a proper TEL platform, and its first launch from a full TEL ensemble took place a year later. Initial deployment began as scheduled in December 1983, along with the Pershing 2s, but there was appreciable opposition from peace protesters and others. Even the government of Denmark suspended monies that had been earmarked to support GLCM deployment.

The Air Force christened the Tomahawk GLCM the Gryphon, naming it for the mythical winged creature with an eagle-like head and the body of a lion. Gryphon crews were trained by the 868th Tactical Missile Training Group at Davis-Monthan Air Force Base, Tucson, Arizona. No Gryphons were based in the United States, however: all were deployed in Western Europe. A total of six sites were assigned. These were known as Main Operating Bases, or MOBs. Listed in the order in which they became operational as GLCM deployment sites, they were: RAF Greenham Common, England (designated MOB-1), where a group of women protesters, maintaining a permanent vigil, came to symbolize the anti-cruise missile movement; Comiso Air Station, Sicily (MOB-2), which was the last site at which GLCMs remained operational; Florennes Air Base, Belgium (MOB-3); Wueschheim Air Station, West Germany (MOB-4); RAF Molesworth, England (MOB-6), which was only operational briefly before the decision was taken to withdraw the GLCMs; and Woensdrecht Air Base, Holland (MOB-5), which did not actually become operational in time to beat the withdrawal.

A Tomahawk cruises to its target during a test flight. The A- and G-variant missiles were accurate to within several hundred feet, sufficient for a nuclear weapon.

Production of Tomahawk GLCMs was halted as a result of the Intermediate-range Nuclear Forces (INF) Treaty, a mutual-security agreement signed by the United States and the Soviet Union in 1987 to remove short-range and medium-range nuclear weapons —those with ranges of 300–3,400 miles (480–5,440km)—from European soil. Under the terms of the treaty, all of the Tomahawk GLCMs and all of the Pershing 2 ballistic missiles that had been deployed in Western Europe were withdrawn and destroyed, as were all of the Soviet Union's nuclear-tipped, triple-warhead SS-20 ballistic missiles deployed in Eastern Europe. In addition, all examples of a Soviet ground-launched cruise missile that had been tested but not deployed at that time would also be destroyed.

The first shipment of Tomahawk GLCMs left West Germany aboard a US Air Force Lockheed C-5 Galaxy on 11 April 1988. There was a public ceremony to mark the occasion, in deference to the fact that the removal of the weapon was a symbolic event to many German citizens. In fact, the GLCMs—removed to Davis-Monthan—were not totally destroyed, as the agreement permitted their engines and guidance systems to be retrieved and employed in the production of A-variant Tomahawk SLCMs. A similar concession was made for the Soviets.

Both sides were permitted on-site inspections to verify destruction of the missiles, and also to make follow-up checks to ensure that no further production was taking place. For example, on 13 February 1989, a ten-person team of Soviet inspectors arrived for a surprise two-day visit to General Dynamics Convair Division's Kearny Mesa plant in San Diego, to verify that activities relating to the Tomahawk GLCM were no longer being conducted there.

Chapter 5

Ship-Attack Tomahawk

The B Variant

There is only one antiship Tomahawk variant. It is known officially as the Conventional Ship-Attack Tomahawk, or TASM (Tomahawk Anti-Ship Missile). Although none were launched in the Gulf War, its intended prey ranges from frigates to what are termed high-value targets: cruisers, destroyers, and aircraft carriers.

A total of 593 B-variant Tomahawks were delivered to the US Navy. Low-rate production began in 1982, and full-rate production got under way in 1984. The final order for B-variant Tomahawks was placed in 1987, and the last missile was delivered in 1989. At the moment of emergence from the launcher, less capsule, but complete with booster, warhead, and a full fuel load, the surface-launched version of the B-variant missile—originally known as the BGM-109B1 but since redesignated RGM-109B—weighs 3,190lb (1,450kg). The submarine-launched version—originally known as the BGM-109B2 but since redesignated UGM-109B—weighs 3,270lb (1,485kg): about 80lb (36kg) more than the surface-launched version, due to the additional weight of its waterproof protective covers and pressure venting device.

The B-variant Tomahawk carries a single 1,000lb (454kg) WDU-25B Bullpup warhead: so-named because it is derived from the warhead carried by the US Air Force's Bullpup air-to-surface missile. The WDU-25B Bullpup is also carried by the C-variant Tomahawk, yet the B variant cannot match the C variant for reach. It can strike targets up to 300 miles (480km) away, whereas the C variant can strike targets up to 700 miles (1,120km) away. This is because, in dealing with mobile targets—the only Tomahawk variant to do so—the B variant has to expend a substantial proportion of its fuel load in a serpentine

In common with all Tomahawk SLCMs, the B variant can be launched underwater. Here, a missile is seen through the parent submarine's periscope as it broaches the surface following a vertical launch.

An antiship Tomahawk with an inert warhead scores a direct hit on a target hulk. The B-variant missile navigates in an altogether different manner to the other variants, because it is the only Tomahawk designed to strike mobile targets. In the time it takes to reach the last known location of its target, the target may have traveled as far as 15 miles (25km).

search pattern. It is, nevertheless, a highly capable weapon. The B-variant Tomahawk has ten times the range of the French Exocet, carries four times the warhead weight, and is at least as accurate.

On 6 December 1976, the first flight of a B-variant Tomahawk took place. As was done during tests of the A variant, it was considered prudent to bypass the boost phase on the early test flights, so the first three flights were air-launched from a US Air Force Boeing B-52. The first launch of a B-variant Tomahawk from a submarine, the USS *Barb*, took place on 2 February 1978.

B-variant missiles became the first Tomahawks to join the US Navy fleet, when they were deployed aboard the renovated Iowa-class battleship USS *New Jersey* in March 1983. They were subsequently deployed aboard a wide variety of Navy vessels.

February 1985 saw the first test flight of a B-variant Tomahawk loaded with a revised software package that allows the missile to undertake the final stages of its mission in a sea-skimming mode. With the introduction of this capability, the B variant was redesignated in the developmental nomenclature: now it was classed as the Block 1A missile, while the B variant with its original capability, along with the A- and G-variant Tomahawks, were henceforth collectively classed as the Block 1 missiles.

In common with the other Tomahawks, the B-variant missile can be launched from either surface vessels or submarines. However, it navigates to its target in an altogether different manner, because in the time it takes to reach the last known location of its target, the target may have traveled as far as 15 miles (25km). The B variant's guidance system is an upgraded version of that installed in the Harpoon antiship missile.

Instead of the inertial guidance set installed aboard the other Tomahawk variants, the B variant's primary source of mid-course guidance is a strapdown three-axis attitude/heading reference system furnished by dual-source suppliers Northrop and Smiths Industries. An identical system is installed aboard the Harpoon. It is better suited to the B-variant's mission than the inertial guidance set fitted to the other Tomahawk variants because it offers a quicker response time (inertial guidance sets require a time-consuming alignment transfer from the parent vessel's inertial navigation system: the operation typically takes 20 minutes).

The strapdown three-axis attitude/heading reference system operates in concert with the same Honeywell radar altimeter installed aboard the other Tomahawk variants, and aboard the Harpoon—although the Harpoon can alternatively carry a Kollsmann-built unit. An IBM digital computer, similar to that installed in the Harpoon, replaces the Litton-built computer fitted to the other Tomahawk variants. However, the B variant's computer has approximately twice the memory of the Harpoon-specification unit, reflecting the fact that the guidance functions of the anti-ship Tomahawk are so much more complex than those of the Harpoon.

The B-variant Tomahawk does not carry either of the navigation-updating systems fitted to the other Tomahawks—neither TERCOM, nor a combination of TERCOM and DSMAC. For one thing, in traversing only a featureless expanse of water, it does not have land-mass contours and other features to help it find its way to the target. More importantly, the Tomahawk does not know precisely where its target is at the time it is launched. Intelligence sources can only indicate the *approximate* range and

bearing of the target at that time.

Instead of TERCOM and TERCOM/DSMAC, therefore, the B-variant Tomahawk has a Texas Instruments active radar seeker, and an IBM passive identification and direction-finding radar receiver, both of which begin operating once the strapdown three-axis attitude/heading reference system has navigated the missile to the designated search region. The missile, having flown from its parent vessel to the search region at an intermediate altitude, climbs just high enough for the passive identification and direction-finding radar receiver and the active radar seeker to perform effectively before commencing its search pattern.

The active radar seeker undertakes the task of locating the enemy ship, sweeping a wide swath back and forth until it eventually locks on, while the passive radar receiver detects and analyzes the ship's radar signals to positively identify it as the target, and in doing so provides correlational data as to which direction the target lies in. By repeating the correlation process several times, the target's precise location can be determined by triangulation.

Once the target ship has been iden-tified and pinpointed, the Tomahawk usually descends to an extremely low altitude: the sea-skimming flight regime. This must be selected prior to launch, and is the preferred method of approac-hing the target, because by hugging the water's surface the Tomahawk has a better chance of eluding the enemy's defenses. Nevertheless, the Tomahawk may rise briefly to a higher altitude to help its active radar seeker get a better fix on the target. The active radar seeker enables the Tomahawk to continue homing-in on the target ship even if the vessel's radar systems are shut down in a belated attempt to avoid passive iden-tification.

Another flight mode that can be

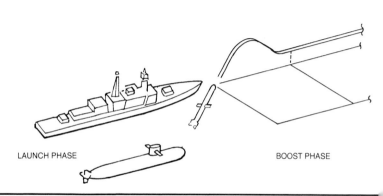

This diagram shows how the B-variant Tomahawk undertakes a serpentine search pattern to locate its target.

LAUNCH PHASE

BOOST PHASE

selected prior to launch is the so-called deceptive maneuver. Under this regime, once it has locked-on to the target using its active radar, the missile alters the direction of its approach to the target, skirting around it. This makes it impossible for the enemy to predict the direction from which the Tomahawk is finally going to strike.

Various other tactics can be employed to deceive the enemy. For example, earlier in the mission, the U-turns within the classical "square" search pattern serve to conceal the location of the missile's parent vessel, as can other types of turns if an alternative search pattern is flown. Such turns are termed search waypoints (not to be confused with the TERCOM waypoints employed by the land-attack Tomahawk variants). If required, search waypoints can also be established outside the search pattern. The Harpoon has similar capabilities, but it employs fewer search waypoints because it has a much shorter range.

The active radar seeker provides guidance right up to the moment of impact, enabling the onboard computer to continuously revise its estimate of the target's location as it steers the missile. Bear in mind that some vessels, destroyers for example, are maneuverable enough to take evasive action. The active radar seeker is an extended-range version of that installed aboard the Harpoon (however, the Harpoon does not have a

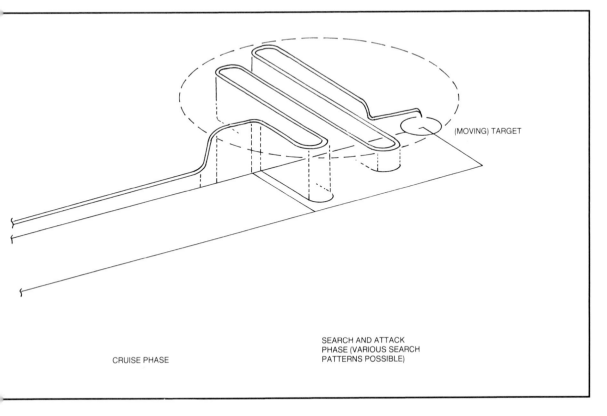

(MOVING) TARGET

CRUISE PHASE

SEARCH AND ATTACK
PHASE (VARIOUS SEARCH
PATTERNS POSSIBLE)

passive system). Although the total pick-up distance remains classified, the improvement in search range is known to be about 250 miles (400km). Of course, there is a risk that emissions from the active radar seeker could be detected by the enemy defenses, making the *Tomahawk* a target. However, an ingenious series of techniques can be employed to foil the enemy and maximize the probability of kill (PK).

As one might expect, these techniques are shrouded in secrecy, but it can be assumed that they exploit known deficiencies in the enemy's ability to track the Tomahawk by its infrared and radar cross-section (RCS) characteristics, and they include a combination of

This stunning photo illustrates the fact that, in employing its active radar seeker to continuously revise its estimate of the aim point, the antiship Tomahawk often strikes at an unusual angle.

the sea-skimming flight regime and the so-called deceptive maneuver.

The B-variant Tomahawk culminates its mission by either broadsiding the target, or by popping-up and diving back down to impact its deck or super-structure. The broadside is the favored mode of attack, because if the missile misses its target for any reason, it can simply turn around and re-attack it.

Although the B-variant Tomahawk has never seen action, it has continually demonstrated its proficiency in test launches. For example, in mid-December 1987, a B-variant Tomahawk—complete with 1,000lb (454kg) Bullpup warhead—successfully located and attacked a target ship hulk in a test at the Pacific Missile Test Center range off the coast of California. The missile was launched vertically from a surface vessel sailing within the range, and flew about 220 miles (350km) to its target.

B-variant missiles became the first Tomahawks to join the US Navy fleet, when they were deployed aboard the renovated Iowa-class battleship USS New Jersey *in March 1983. Here, a missile blasts away from a surface vessel's armored box launcher.*

Chapter 6

Tomahawks in the Gulf War

The C and D Variants

Operation Desert Storm marked the Tomahawk's first use under combat conditions. It was also significant in being the first occasion that cruise missiles were used in conjunction with manned air strikes, a capability that had not even been demonstrated in military exercises. The Tomahawk proved devastatingly effective in the Gulf War, achieving a hit rate in excess of 90 percent. Two Tomahawk variants saw action in the conflict: the C- and D-variant missiles. Before reviewing their exploits, we will examine the missiles themselves, starting with the C variant.

The C-variant missile is officially titled the Conventional Land-Attack Tomahawk, or TLAM-C (Tomahawk Land Attack Missile-C). It is intended to neutralize high-value, heavily-defended targets, and the defensive systems themselves, or to soften them prior to attacks by manned aircraft, the latter reducing the risk to the aircraft and their pilots. The C-variant missile has a range of 700 miles (1,120km), and carries a single 1,000lb (454kg) WDU-25B Bullpup warhead—the same warhead carried by the B-variant, antiship Tomahawk.

When it first emerged, the C variant was classified in the developmental nomenclature as the Block 2 missile. It entered US Navy service in 1986, thereby becoming the third Tomahawk SLCM variant to achieve operational status.

The C variant is the heaviest member of the Tomahawk family. At the moment of emergence from the launcher, less capsule, but complete with booster, warhead, and a full fuel load, the surface-launched version of the C-variant missile —originally known as the BGM-109C1 but since redesignated RGM-109C— weighs 3,435lb (1,560kg). The submarine-launched version—originally known as the BGM-109C2 but since redesignated

The C variant is the heaviest member of the Tomahawk family.

Launch from an Iowa-class battleship. The C variant entered US Navy service in 1986, thereby becoming the third Tomahawk SLCM variant to achieve operational status. It undertook the lion's share of Tomahawk strikes in the Gulf War, achieving a hit rate in excess of 90 percent.

C-variant Tomahawks can undertake any one of three alternative modes of attack. Pictured here is the horizontal attack man- *euver (HAM), in which the missile flies directly into the side of the target—usually a building—in a horizontal attitude.*

UGM-109C—weighs 3,300lb (1,500kg) at launch: 135lb (61kg) less than the surface-launched version, despite the fact that it carries protective covers and a pressure-venting device. This is because the submarine-launched version does not carry a full fuel load. It is simply too heavy to be launched fully-fueled from the maximum permitted depth.

During Operation Desert Storm, C-variant Tomahawks struck such targets as the central intelligence facility in Baghdad, key communications sites, and buildings occupied by the ministry of defense, ahead of strikes by US Air Force Lockheed F-117 stealth attack bombers and other attack aircraft. Naval bases and airfields are also typical C-variant Tomahawk targets.

In the terminal phase of its mission, the C-variant Tomahawk can undertake any one of three alternative modes of attack. The desired mode must be selected prior to launch, and is related to the nature of the target and/or the nature of the environment in which the target is situated. In the first potential attack mode, known as the horizontal attack maneuver (HAM), the missile flies directly into the side of the target—usually a building of some kind—in a horizontal attitude. This was the original C-variant attack mode.

In the second potential attack mode, known as the pop-up/terminal-dive maneuver, the missile enters a climb just before reaching the target—again, usually a building—then rolls through 180 deg-

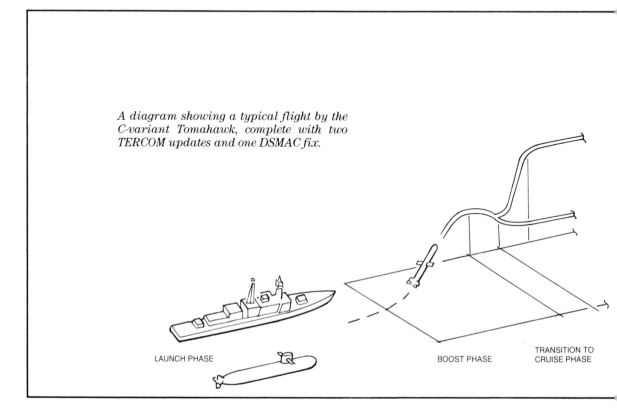

A diagram showing a typical flight by the C-variant Tomahawk, complete with two TERCOM updates and one DSMAC fix.

LAUNCH PHASE

BOOST PHASE

TRANSITION TO CRUISE PHASE

rees and dives down to impact the top of the target in a near-vertical attitude. Although this mode of attack has parallels with the pop-up attack option that the B-variant, antiship Tomahawk can exercise, the two maneuvers should not be confused. The very fact that a ship is a moving target means that there is a fundamental difference between the geometries of the two maneuvers.

The pop-up/terminal-dive maneuver was facilitated solely by a software change, and this is characteristic of what has been done throughout the history of the Tomahawk program. The aim has been to make the hardware as universally capable as possible, then add specific performance features through software changes. Software refinements

are obviously much easier and more cost-effective to implement than hardware modifications. Once the software for a new flight program has been developed, it is only necessary to create as many copies as there are launch platforms. When a launch platform loads a revised program into a Tomahawk's onboard computer, that missile immediately has the new capability, without any other work being performed. in short, the missile has been instantaneously modified.

With the introduction of the software change that facilitated the pop-up/terminal-dive maneuver, the C-variant Tomahawk was redesignated in the developmental nomenclature: now it was classed as the Block 2A missile.

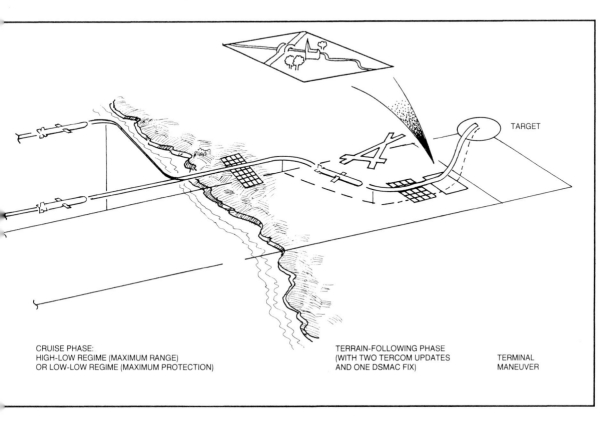

CRUISE PHASE:
HIGH-LOW REGIME (MAXIMUM RANGE)
OR LOW-LOW REGIME (MAXIMUM PROTECTION)

TERRAIN-FOLLOWING PHASE
(WITH TWO TERCOM UPDATES
AND ONE DSMAC FIX)

TERMINAL
MANEUVER

TARGET

The pop-up/terminal-dive maneuver is an alternative attack mode for the C-variant Tomahawk. The missile enters a climb just before reaching the target, then rolls through 180 degrees and dives down to impact the top of the target in a near-vertical attitude.

In the C variant's third potential attack mode, known as the programmed warhead detonation (PWD) maneuver, the missile flies over the top of the target, then detonates the Bullpup warhead directly above it, showering it with shrapnel. As a general rule, the PWD maneuver is employed against targets that have some type of physical shielding, be it man-made protection—as is the case with a revetted aircraft—or a natural form of defense, such as a row of trees.

Whichever mode of attack is selected, the required maneuvers are governed by the Tomahawk's onboard computer, which commands the appropriate control surface movements. Like the rest of a Tomahawk's mission, the commands necessary to enact the maneuver are programmed in by mission planners before the missile is launched, and are based on a comprehensive knowledge of the target and its defenses.

The D-variant missile—officially titled

This Rockwell RA-5 Vigilante target hulk, seemingly safe in a revetment, is about to fall prey to a C-variant Tomahawk employing a mode of attack known as the programmed warhead detonation (PWD) maneuver. The

missile flies over the top of the target, then detonates its 1,000lb (454kg) Bullpup warhead directly above it, showering it with shrapnel.

the Submunition Land-Attack Tomahawk, or TLAM-D (Tomahawk Land
Attack Missile-D)—is a direct derivative
of the C-variant Tomahawk. In fact, with
the exception of a reconfigured payload
section, it is identical, although the re-
configuration results in it weighing
somewhat less. At the moment of emergence from the launcher, less capsule,
but complete with booster, warhead,
and a full fuel load, the surface-launched
version of the D-variant missile—originally
known as the BGM-109D1 but since
redesignated RGM-109D—weighs 3,230lb
(1,465kg). The submarine-launched version—originally known as the BGM-109D2
but since redesignated UGM-109D—
weighs 3,330lb (1,510kg), complete with
its protective covers and the pressure-

venting device.

Within the revised payload section,
in place of the single 1,000lb (454kg)
Bullpup warhead carried by the C-variant
Tomahawk, the D variant has a submunition dispenser loaded with 166
individual bomblets, each about the size
of soft-drink can. These BLU-97/B Combined Effects Bomblets (CEBs) can be
dispensed at intervals in partial batches,
to destroy multiple targets as the missile
overflies them: for example, groupings
of aircraft parked on taxiways, or in
revetments. Missile storage sites, radar
installations, and other such targets are
equally vulnerable to CEBs.

Each bomblet is 6.6in (16.8cm) long,
2.5in (6.3cm) in diameter, and 3.4lb
(1.5kg) in weight. The term "combined-

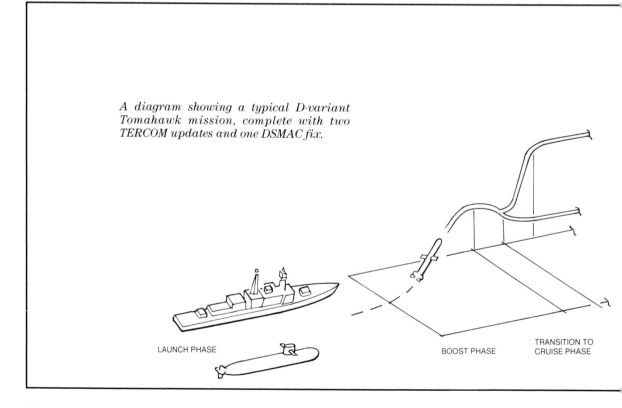

A diagram showing a typical D-variant Tomahawk mission, complete with two TERCOM updates and one DSMAC fix.

LAUNCH PHASE

BOOST PHASE

TRANSITION TO CRUISE PHASE

effects" is a reference to the fact that each bomblet has a combined armor-piercing/fragmentation/incendiary capability, making it effective against a variety of targets. There are twenty-four batches of CEBs, twenty-two of which comprise seven bomblets and two of which comprise six bomblets. The CEBs are dispensed in equal quantities right and left, so as not to upset the missile's balance in flight.

When it first emerged, the D variant was classified in the developmental nomenclature as the Block 2B missile. Following a comprehensive test program, it achieved Initial Operational Capability (IOC) in 1986, thereby becoming the fourth Tomahawk SLCM variant to reach operational status. Over 1,100 have been built to date, and twenty-seven were launched during Operation Desert Storm.

Until they get close to the target area, both the C- and D-variant Tomahawks navigate in the same manner as the nuclear-tipped A variant described in Chapter 4, making their way over water and land with the aid of a Litton inertial guidance set, a Honeywell radar altimeter, and TERCOM (a terrain-matching software subsystem that functions within the onboard Litton digital computer). In the terminal phase of their mission, however, another system—the Digital Scene-Matching Area Correlator (DSMAC)—takes over the task of updating the guidance system. Its function is to refine the accuracy of the flight path still further, because con-

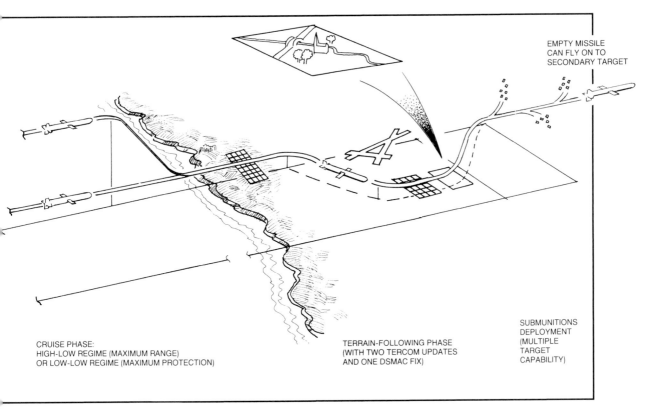

EMPTY MISSILE CAN FLY ON TO SECONDARY TARGET

CRUISE PHASE:
HIGH-LOW REGIME (MAXIMUM RANGE)
OR LOW-LOW REGIME (MAXIMUM PROTECTION)

TERRAIN-FOLLOWING PHASE
(WITH TWO TERCOM UPDATES
AND ONE DSMAC FIX)

SUBMUNITIONS
DEPLOYMENT
(MULTIPLE
TARGET
CAPABILITY)

ventional warheads require more much precise delivery than nuclear warheads.

Housed in the Tomahawk's nose (guidance section), the DSMAC is an electro-optical sensor system that collects images of distinctive ground features, both natural and man-made, and processes them into digital form. The missile's onboard computer then compares these images with images of the same features stored in its memory. Each comparison is analogous to overlaying a theoretical map over an actual one, and indicates to the guidance system how much adjust-

ment must be made to the flight path at that specific point to maintain the correct course. By this method (known as offset navigation: the technique of looking at one thing to go somewhere else), the missile orients itself for the final run to the target.

There are two elements to the DSMAC: a receiver-processor unit (RPU) and an illuminator device. The latter produces a momentary strobe-like flash that illuminates the ground by night. According to eyewitnesses, in darkness the flashes are clearly visible. DSMAC

A Vought F-8 Crusader target hulk under attack from a D-variant Tomahawk. This variant has a submunition dispenser loaded with 166 individual bomblets, each about the size of soft-drink can. These BLU-97/B

Combined Effects Bomblets (CEBs) can be dispensed at intervals in partial batches, to destroy multiple targets as the missile over-flies them.

scenes (also called maps) are known to be much smaller than TERCOM maps, but the precise dimensions are secret. Like TERCOM maps, the DSMAC scenes become progressively smaller as the target is approached, honing the accuracy of the flight path. While TERCOM maps are rectangular in shape and are employed in a series of groupings known collectively as a map set, DSMAC scenes are square and are employed singly. In a typical strike, either two or three DSMAC scenes are employed. However, at no stage in the scene-matching process does the missile look at its target. It always looks directly downward.

As with TERCOM maps, DSMAC scenes are selected by mission planners prior to launch, employing data supplied by the Defense Mapping Agency (DMA) and other intelligence sources, including reconnaissance satellite imagery. The reference imagery is loaded into the Tomahawk's computer in digital form on a disk, along with all of the other mission data. When selecting suitable DSMAC scenes, mission planners must ensure that each scene has some *distinctive* and *unambiguous* features that can serve as reference points. A scene containing a road junction, or a bridge over a railway line, is likely to meet the mission planners' criteria. Waterways and woodland areas, with their distinctive shapes, could also serve as key features in DSMAC scenes.

However, since DSMAC is an optical system, care must be taken to ensure that the key features of the scene will not be significantly altered if seasonal, meteorological or other factors intervene. For example, during winter in many countries, waterways can get iced-over, then covered in a thick layer of snow, in which case they would fail to register with the DSMAC. Parking lots and other such features can also dis-appear under a snow covering.

As one might expect, the database from which DSMAC scenes are selected is regularly updated, because features can change over time. Buildings can be extended, or even demolished, the boundaries of woodland areas can be altered by tree felling, and so on. Intelligence sources monitor such activity in relevant areas and ensure that the database is amended accordingly. Satellite imagery is particularly useful in this regard. There are very few places in the world so featureless that they would offer no scenes for the DSMAC to work from. In those places, obviously, the Tomahawk would be unsuitable and a different weapon system would have to be used.

Thanks to DSMAC, the C-variant Tomahawk, in particular, is one of the most accurate weapons in service in the world today. Its accuracy is such that, after undertaking a journey to its maximum range of 700 miles (1,120km), it could fly through the goalposts at both ends of a football field. DSMAC was

Remains of the Crusader after the submunitions have done their work.

developed by the Naval Avionics Center (now the Naval Air Warfare Center—Aircraft Division) in Indianapolis, Indiana. DSMAC systems for the Tomahawk are manufactured by McDonnell Douglas, at its St. Louis, Missouri, plant.

To limit destruction if the Tomahawk strays off-course on its way to the target, mission planners predesignate a particular point along the route as the point at which the onboard computer arms the warhead. Unless the missile has achieved a successful navigation update prior to reaching the predesignated point, the warhead will not be armed. The decision as to how far along the route the arming point should lie is based upon several factors, all of which are carefully assessed and are the subject of a well-defined set of rules. Naturally, it's safest to arm the warhead as near as possible to the target.

While the C-variant Tomahawk concludes its mission by undertaking one of three alternative modes of attack, and is destroyed in the process, the D-variant Tomahawk can conclude its mission in a very different manner. For, having attacked its target, it lives to fight on. Although its flying qualities are somewhat diminished by the center-of-gravity shift that occurs when it dispenses its munitions, the unarmed missile is still capable of flying to a secondary target and crashing into it. Even devoid of explosives, the missile has sufficient mass—including the residual fuel load—to cause considerable damage. For this purpose, the D variant possesses the same pop-up/terminal-dive capability as the C variant, although it can also fly directly into the target, horizontally (the HAM mode, described previously). The empty missile can also serve as a decoy on its way to the secondary target, provoking the enemy to expend its defensive missiles. In both cases, the decision as to which action should be taken must be made prior to launch, and the missile programmed accordingly.

A D-variant Tomahawk pictured with its submunition payload covers jettisoned. After it has released its submunitions on the primary target, the empty missile can fly to a secondary target and crash into it.

Into action

Operation Desert Storm began in the early-morning darkness of 17 January 1991, when fifty-two Tomahawks were launched from various surface vessels in the Red Sea and the Persian Gulf. All were C-variant Tomahawks, and all but one struck their target.

The fact that the Tomahawk was employed to spearhead hostilities against Iraq not only underscored the rationale behind this potent cruise missile, but also attests to the high level of confidence the military planners had in its capabilities. This unexpected wave of strikes had made the most of the cruise missile's unique capabilities, being directed at targets which demanded a high level of precision, and at targets protected by the heaviest antiaircraft defenses. The Tomahawks hit the Iraqi presidential palace, ministry of defense buildings, and a central communications facility in Baghdad. Fixed Iraqi air-defense systems were also targeted. In most cases, two Tomahawks were assigned to each aim point, allowing the second missile to achieve greater penetration.

Another use to which Tomahawks were put in the opening hours of Operation Desert Storm was the delivery of a novel form of *non-lethal* weaponry. Iraq's centrally controlled air defense facilities depended on the commercial electricity generating and distribution network to operate radar antennas, computers that integrated the air defense network, and vital communications equipment. Special warheads filled with thousands of small spools of a very fine carbon fiber wire were showered onto the outdoor switching and transformer areas of Iraq's major electrical facilities, causing massive short circuits and overloads that temporarily disabled the country's air defenses, allowing radar and surface-to-air missile sites to be destroyed by air strikes almost at will. According to a DoD spokesperson, the Tomahawks in question were "specially-built TLAMs." If this is the case, it is likely that they were directly derived from the D-variant missile.

One key benefit of this type of attack is that the civilian population, who relied on the same electrical facilities for their domestic needs, were only disrupted for a few days while repairs were effected. Generating equipment, although shut down by the short circuits, was not permanently damaged.

With the Iraqi defenses "blinded" by the disrupted electricity supply, other tactics were employed to cause further confusion. One tactic that deserves particular mention was the combined use of Tomahawks and Northrop BQM-74 drones to fool the Iraqis into believing that allied bombers were attacking Baghdad. The pre-programmed drones flew in formations of three or four, to imitate a wave of bombers in flight, then flew in circles and figure eights while Tomahawks stuck key targets below. This created the illusion that the drones were bombers and the exploding Tomahawks were falling bombs.

With one exception, it was not indicated which vessels had launched the first wave of Tomahawks. Only the involvement of the Iowa-class battleship USS *Wisconsin* (BB-64) was acknowledged. Her sister ship, the Tomahawk-toting USS *Missouri* (BB-63), was known to be operating in the Persian Gulf at that time, as were at least four or five Tomahawk-equipped cruisers, while eight cruisers armed with Tomahawks were known to have been operating in the Red Sea at that time.

Discussing the first strikes, Colin Powell, chairman of the US Joint Chiefs of Staff, said that he "was very pleased with the effectiveness of the cruise missiles." Powell's favorable remarks, and the deeds that drew them, were a boost to proponents of cruise missiles. Prior to the outbreak of hostilities in the Gulf, doubters had expressed concerns that the Tomahawk—which had never been fired in large numbers, or in combat, before—may not be capable of striking targets accurately in anything less than perfect conditions. In particular, there were concerns that the missile would be unable to navigate properly in darkness: a legacy of the early stages of the Tomahawk's development, when the DSMAC terminal navigation system had failed to perform as expected at night.

That initial attack set the tone for subsequent Tomahawk successes. In the first two weeks of the campaign, only C-variant Tomahawks were used—about 250 in all, accounting for rather less than one-quarter of the Navy's total inventory of that variant: about 900. With one exception, all were fired from the armored box launchers or vertical launch systems of about a dozen surface vessels operating in the Persian Gulf and the Red Sea. Only one Tomahawk had been fired by a submarine up to that point. The submarine in question was

A warehouse-sized target is destroyed by a C-variant Tomahawk at the culmination of a test mission, graphically demonstrating the missile's lethality. The concrete slabs from which the building was composed were numbered to aid photographic analysis. Each slab weighs 7,000lb (3,180kg).

operating in the Red Sea.

In the latter stages of the campaign, D-variant Tomahawks were also put to work. They were employed against soft targets such as aircraft parked in revetments, motor pools, and large concentrations of troops.

During the Gulf War, some members of the allied forces encountered the *enemy's* cruise missiles: Iraqi's Chinese-built HY-2 Silkworms. A British Royal Navy Type 42 destroyer, HMS *Gloucester*, shot down a Silkworm while sailing in the Persian Gulf, about 20 miles (32km) offshore. The Silkworm was intercepted about 4 miles (6.4km) from the *Gloucester* by a British Aerospace Sea Dart medium-range, air-to-air missile. Silkworms cruise at an altitude of about 1,000ft (305m), then commence a step-down descent to their targets. Apparently, this particular Silkworm had already begun its descent when the Sea Dart struck it.

By the end of the first week of February, nearly 300 Tomahawks had been launched against Iraqi targets. With Tomahawks being expended at such a rate, it was inevitable that the US Navy would request further supplies. In early February, the Office of the US Secretary of Defense approved a request for 400 additional Tomahawks under the Fiscal Year 1991 Tomahawk weapons procurement (funding was approved by Congress some months later), and also gave its support to the service's request for the delivery of Tomahawks being manufactured under the Fiscal Year 1989 purchase to be accelerated.

Saddam Hussain's regime was not toppled by the allied onslaught, merely chastised. Some of the conditions laid down by the United Nations when the cease-fire was brokered remained unfulfilled: primarily, the dismantling of the means of production of weapons of mass destruction. In the first week of August 1991, Navy mission planners, anticipating renewed strikes against Iraq, completed the task of retargeting Tomahawks at key sites identified since hostilities ceased. Likely targets included research, manufacturing, and storage facilities for nuclear, biological, and chemical weapons.

Mission planners also corrected an impediment that had earlier prevented some Tomahawks from locating their targets. Ironically, the problem had resulted from the *success* of earlier air strikes. The destruction of certain key buildings had made it difficult for the Tomahawks' DSMAC terminal guidance systems to identify the missiles' routes to their targets. To alleviate the problem, mission planners created alternate routes for future strikes that would keep the missiles away from areas that had been heavily bombed.

It was some time before Tomahawks were again unleashed against Iraq. Only after numerous unsuccessful attempts to secure Iraqi compliance with United Nations mandates was the order issued for Tomahawks to strike the Zaafaraniyah nuclear fabrication facility, suspected of being engaged in nuclear weapons development. The attack took place on 17 January 1993. (An interesting aside: the cost of the Zaafaraniyah raid was put at $45–60 million—a little over $1 million per Tomahawk). Of the forty-five Tomahawks launched, 18 percent failed to hit their assigned aim points. Although the Pentagon's projected 80–85 percent success rate had been achieved, questions arose as to why such a comparatively large proportion of the missiles had failed to hit their targets.

The US Navy, conducting preliminary investigations into the Zaafaraniyah raid, ascertained that seven errant missiles either impacted fields close to the nuclear fabrication facility, or came down within the perimeter of the facility, but short of the target itself. The investigators postulated that some Tomahawks may have failed to hit their targets because of tiny measuring errors made by mission planners as they prepared targeting data, thereby causing the missiles to undertake incorrect DSMAC guidance updates in the final seconds prior to impact. Specifically, it was discovered that a minute misalignment of the aim point on a film image of the target area, the result of something as apparently trivial as an item of mission planning hardware being jarred slightly, would be sufficient to cause the missile to miss its target by several hundred yards.

By the time the next Tomahawk strike took place against an Iraqi target—the central intelligence headquarters in Baghdad, five months later, on 26 June 1993—a new, digital mission planning system had been adopted in place of the manual one. Despite this precaution, an higher percentage of missiles—33 percent of the twenty-three Tomahawks launched on this raid—failed to hit their assigned aim points. A twenty-fourth Tomahawk assigned to the raid was not launched, due to a malfunction arising in its navigation system. Subsequent analysis revealed that sixteen of the Tomahawks had hit their aim points, three came down within the perimeter of the intelligence facility (but short of the target itself), one landed in a manner that rendered accurate identification of the impact point impossible, and three impacted in a residential area close to the target.

Although the success rate for this mission, at 67 percent, fell within the bounds deemed acceptable for unmanned systems, an investigation was conducted to ascertain why the exceptionally high standards set by earlier Tomahawk missions had not been achieved. Every one of the errant Tomahawks had impacted within a few hundred yards of the target, so there appeared to be some correlation between the failures.

Eventually, investigators concluded that two factors had probably contributed to the poor success rate achieved on the 26 June raid. First, it appeared likely that malfunctioning flight control actuators caused missiles to alter course slightly in the critical final moments of flight, missing their target by a small margin.

The other factor was the heavy antiaircraft fire encountered during the final run-in to the target. On this occasion, antiaircraft crews had a relatively easy task firing at the incoming Tomahawks, because they all approached the target from the same direction. This, in turn, resulted from a shortage of adequate TERCOM waypoints in the largely featureless desert, which severely limited the available routes to Baghdad. The two streams of Tomahawks—launched from US Navy vessels positioned in the Red Sea and the Persian Gulf—merged over the outskirts of Baghdad, not far from the target. With successive Tomahawks appearing along the same route, the enemy gunners were able to perfect their aim while directing fire at them as they popped up over the target, rolled over and dove steeply down. Only the first missile benefitted from the element of surprise.

Following its successes in the Gulf, one suspects that if the need arises for Tomahawks to be employed in anger again, even greater use will be made of its unique capabilities.

Chapter 7

Into the Future

Upgrading the Tomahawk

Because technological advancement is unceasing, if the lethality of a weapon system is to be maintained, it must be periodically upgraded. The Tomahawk is no exception. In December 1988, the US Navy awarded McDonnell Douglas Missile Systems Company a $165 million contract to develop a comprehensive upgrade to three of the four elements of the Tomahawk Weapons System (TWS) —every element except the Launching System. As well as improving performance and flexibility, the upgrades would reduce the onerous workload required to plan Tomahawk strikes.

Not only were new C- and D-variant Tomahawks to be built to this upgraded standard—which was to be known as Block 3 specification—but existing C- and D-variant Tomahawks were to be similarly upgraded when they came in for periodic overhaul.

McDonnell Douglas Missiles Systems Company and General Dynamics Convair Division had competed for the contract to undertake engineering and development of the Block 3 upgrades. When McDonnell Douglas won, it entrusted the task to its St. Louis, Missouri plant. Thereafter, as with earlier Tomahawks, production of Block 3 models was to be undertaken in parallel by McDonnell Douglas Missile Systems Company at its Titusville, Florida, facility, and by General Dynamics Convair Division at its Kearny Mesa site in San Diego, California, under an annual competitive procurement program.

Four years later, in August 1992,

while production of Block 3 Tomahawks was in progress, all of the missile programs of General Dynamics Convair Division were acquired by Hughes Missile Systems Company of Tucson, Arizona. Soon after, Hughes transferred its newly-acquired Tomahawk production capability to Tucson. There were less radical changes at McDonnell Douglas Missile Systems Company: under a corporate reorganization program, this operating division became McDonnell Douglas Aerospace-East in 1992.

The Block 3 upgrade effort was well under way by the time the Gulf War broke out, but the improved missile had not reached a sufficient state of readiness to see action in that conflict.

Block 3 Tomahawks incorporate the following refinements:

■ Software, and some hardware, upgrades that allow faster mission planning. The Block 3 mission planning upgrades took advantage of the boom in computational power over the preceding decade and of the enormous improvements in the quality of computer-generated displays, to undertake data management much more rapidly, and to automate many routine mission planning tasks.

One example of the way in which automatic processes have supplanted laborious manual tasks is the streamlined method by which a mission planner sets the altitudes a Tomahawk will fly at en route to its target. As related in Chapter 4, a key element of this task is achieving a balance between flying too high, thereby risking detection by enemy radars and the attendant possibility of being shot down by enemy ground defenses, and flying too low, thereby risking a crash. In the very early days of the Tomahawk program, a mission planner plotted the ground track with little more than "pencil and paper" technology, using the elevation data (contour lines) on a topographic map to calculate the altitudes required to maintain a safe ground clearance. Although, over time, this process became computerized, it was still unwieldy and time-consuming.

Now, with the Block 3 upgrades, once a relatively small amount of infor-

A Tomahawk soars heavenward. As well as improving performance and flexibility, the Block 3 upgrades have reduced the onerous workload required to plan Tomahawk strikes.

mation has been entered into a database, two software architectures—one known as the auto router, the other known as a vertical profile generator—combine to automatically generate the ground track and the appropriate vertical profile respectively. Other vital parameters, such as flight speeds, are also automatically calculated. These data are subsequently loaded into the Tomahawk's on-board Litton digital computer.

■ New software that can implement route deviations to either shorten or lengthen the missile's flight path, in order to attain a predesignated arrival time at the target. Bearing in mind that Tomahawks were designed to complement carrier-based aircraft, there has long been a concern that the manned aircraft might arrive over the target area at the same time as the Tomahawks and suffer damage as a result. Being able to accurately predict when the Tomahawks will arrive at their targets will facilitate greater precision in coordinating joint air strikes by Tomahawks and manned aircraft. The new software is known as Time of Arrival (TOA) control.

■ An upgraded version of the DSMAC-2 terminal guidance system, designated DSMAC-2A. (The DSMAC system, as described in Chapter 6 and installed aboard operational C- and D-variant Tomahawks prior to the Block 3 upgrade program, is actually designated DSMAC-2. The designation DSMAC, without suffix, was applied only to a prototype system installed aboard test examples of the C-variant missile. Thus, the new version is designated DSMAC-2A).

DSMAC-2A incorporates improvements both in hardware and software, enabling it to use as many as 50 percent more scenes than the previous system. For example, it can distinguish features in conditions of low visual contrast, such as those encountered in the Middle East, where plain buildings are situated in sandy surroundings. Similarly, it is better at coping with the potentially confusing visual effects that result from diurnal (day/night) cycles and seasonal changes (snow, for instance, or foliage), both of which can alter the appearance of buildings and landscapes.

Thus, the DSMAC-2A system improves operational flexibility on two counts: by providing mission planners with 50 percent more scenes to choose from, it enables them to undertake their work more rapidly; and the increased number of potential waypoints widens their choice of available strike routes.

■ A receiver that enables it to operate in conjunction with the Navstar Global Positioning System (GPS), a "constellation" of Earth-orbiting navigation satellites. Any aircraft, waterborne vessel or land vehicle equipped with a GPS receiver can determine its spatial position to within a few yards, and also determine its velocity (speed and direction), simply by triangulating the radio signals these satellites broadcast continuously, 24 hours a day.

It will be recalled from earlier chapters that land-attack Tomahawk variants employ a software subsystem known as Terrain Contour Matching, TERCOM, to help them navigate to their targets. At predetermined points (waypoints) along the intended route, TERCOM compares terrain profiles gathered by the missile's Honeywell radar altimeter with digital terrain maps of the corresponding regions stored in the on-board computer (the latter are based on data gathered by intelligence sources), updating the inertial guidance system and implementing the required course corrrections. Under most circumstances, Block 3 Tomahawks will employ GPS to supplement TERCOM, as that can allow certain waypoints to be bypassed, and in any event provides an additional guarantee of accuracy.

In certain cases, GPS could substitute completely for TERCOM, serving as an alternative means of navigation: for example, if the need arose to strike at short notice a target for which no TERCOM data was available. Extensive flight path imagery is required for TERCOM guidance, and gathering and processing it takes a great deal of time. Navigating to a target solely by GPS has the advantage of eliminating the need for such extensive imagery, greatly decreasing the time expended on mission planning, possibly reducing it to only a few hours. DSMAC data will still be required, because for all its capabilities, GPS cannot surpass the DSMAC system for accuracy.

Another example of when GPS could be employed as a substitute for TERCOM is for attacks against certain coastal targets. In the past, a Tomahawk launched to strike a coastal target would have had to fly over land to orient itself before making its run-in to the target, but the Block 3 model—using only its GPS link—could attack directly from the sea. The only time this would not be feasible is if an extremely high degree of accuracy was required, in which case the Tomahawk would still have to fly over land briefly, in order to obtain a high-accuracy DSMAC fix.

Other situations can be cited as examples. An obvious one is prolonged flight over featureless terrain. GPS guidance would have greatly improved the success rate of the Tomahawk strike against the Iraqi central intelligence headquarters in Baghdad on 26 June 1993 (as described in Chapter 6), because it would have freed the Tomahawks of their reliance on the few-and-far-between waypoints in the virtually featureless desert, enabling them to approach the target from several different directions, and thereby tax the Iraqi gunners.

As with all GPS receivers employed for military purposes, those installed aboard Block 3 Tomahawks are modified to increase their resistance to enemy jamming.

■ A greater fuel capacity, increasing the range by about 30 percent. Note that this applies only to the C-variant Tomahawk: the D variant's range remains the same.

The C variant's range was increased by as much as 300 miles (480km)—from 700 miles (1,120km) to 900–1,000 miles (1,440–1,600km)—by installing a smaller and lighter warhead, and making changes to the configuration of the payload section to enable extra fuel to be carried. Designated WDU-36B, the new warhead creates the same blast effect as the 1,000lb (454kg) WDU-25B Bullpup, yet weighs only 700lb (318kg), allowing about 230lb (105kg) of additional fuel to be stored around it. It was developed at the Naval Weapons Center, China Lake, California, and is an insensitive warhead (meaning that it can only be detonated by its timing fuze, and will therefore not explode in the presence of heat and flame in the event of an accidental impact). It has a programmable delay fuze, allowing the detonation to be timed to assure maximum destruction. For example, in a horizontal attack, it may be desirable to have the warhead explode several milliseconds after penetrating an exterior wall, to ensure that it has passed through one or more interior walls before exploding. Similarly, in an attack from above, it may be desirable for the missile to penetrate to a specific floor before the warhead detonates.

IW/ER is the designation applied to the Block 3-specification payload section of the C-variant Tomahawk. The initials stand for Insensitive Warhead/Extended Range.

■ Although not strictly part of the Block 3 upgrade program, the opportunity is being taken to install an improved version of the Williams International F107 turbofan engine in the all-new Block 3 Tomahawks. Existing missiles, when they come in for periodic overhaul and receive the Block 3 upgrades, are also receiving this improved engine.

Designated F107-WR-402, the new engine develops 19 percent more thrust under hot day conditions, and 10 percent more thrust under all other conditions, combined with a 3 percent decrease in fuel consumption. The increase in thrust was expected to alleviate a concern that surfaced some time after the Block 3 upgrades were defined—during the Gulf War, in fact—that Tomahawks routed through mountainous regions on hot days might "run out of breath."

In addition to the modifications that improved flight performance, the Dash 402 engine incorporates modifications that double the engine recertification interval to six years, reducing maintenance and missile down-time.

■ Again, although not strictly part of the Block 3 upgrade program, the opportunity is being taken to fit an increased-thrust solid rocket booster to every all-new C-variant missile destined for submarine deployment. The more powerful booster will also be retrofitted to existing submarine-based C-variant Tomahawks when they come in for periodic overhaul and receive the Block 3 upgrades. The intention is to overcome a performance deficiency of the Type 106 booster, which had insufficient thrust to allow the C-variant missile—the heaviest member of the Tomahawk family—to be launched fully-fueled from maximum permitted depths. With the new booster, submarine-launched C-variant Tomahawks can achieve the same range as those launched from surface vessels.

The new booster is designated Type 111. Like the standard Type 106 booster, it is manufactured by dual-source suppliers Atlantic Research and United Technologies. Block 3 missiles destined for deployment on surface vessels continue to be fitted with the Type 106 booster.

All of the modifications listed above had to be thoroughly tested in flight before the Block 3 Tomahawk could be declared operational. Teething troubles are to be expected with any new weapon system, and the Block 3 Tomahawk was no exception. The first flight test took place on 15 January 1991—coincidentally, less than 48 hours before the outbreak of the Gulf War. The Tomahawk, a C-variant missile, was launched vertically from a permanent pad on San Nicholas Island in the Pacific Missile Test Center range off Southern California. There were no problems with the launch, but during the flight, things went awry.

The Tomahawk was supposed to fly 700 miles (1,120km) to a target area at the Naval Weapons Test Center, China Lake, but the flight had to be curtailed at an early stage when problems in software linking the GPS receiver with the missile's guidance system caused anomalies. Test engineers elected to take control of the missile and flew it to San Clemente Island, some 50 miles (80km) off Los Angeles, where it was successfully retrieved.

With the software problem rectified, the exercise was repeated on 13 February 1991, with much better results. During the 90-minute flight to China Lake, many of the Block 3 upgrades—including the GPS receiver, the DSMAC-2A terminal guidance system, and the time-of-arrival control function—were

Under the Block 3 upgrade program, all C-variant missiles destined for submarine deployment are being fitted with an uprated booster rocket. This enables the heaviest member of the Tomahawk family to be launched fully-fueled from maximum permitted depths.

put through their paces, as were the Dash 402 engine upgrades. The new WDU-36B warhead and fuze were not tested on this occasion, however.

In May of that year, another important event took place: the first launch of a Block 3 Tomahawk from the torpedo tube of a submerged, moving submarine. Again, the launch was made from the Pacific Test Range and culminated in a 1 hour, 25 minute flight to China Lake, where the missile was recovered.

On 13 November 1991, the first launching of a Block 3 Tomahawk with a live WDU-36B warhead took place. The missile was vertically launched from the USS *David R. Ray*, while sailing off the coast of California. The target was a building located on San Clemente Island. The Tomahawk completed its mission with a successful terminal dive into the target.

The US Navy completed operational test flights of the Block 3 Tomahawk in February 1992 (developmental test flights are conducted in conjunction with the contractor, while operational test flights are a follow-on series of tests conducted solely by the service). Full-rate production was approved that July.

Another milestone was passed on 2 September 1992, when the Navy successfully completed the first operational test launch of a Block 3 Tomahawk from a Block 3-specification Tomahawk Weapon Control System (TWCS) platform—the latest version of the shipboard hardware/software ensemble that supports Tomahawk missions—thereby clearing the way for the missile to avail itself of the whole gamut of Block 3 performance upgrades. The test was conducted from the cruiser USS *Arkansas*, at the Pacific Missile Test Center range off the California coast. The route planned for the missile featured a total of five waypoints: GPS updates were provided in lieu of TERCOM updates, and all of the DSMAC-2A updates were successful. After an autonomous flight that lasted over one hour, the Tomahawk flew over the target, and was successfully recovered at the Naval Air Weapons Center at China Lake.

On 9 March 1993, the first Block 3 Tomahawk was delivered to the US Navy, and IOC was achieved in May of that year.

All of the Tomahawks expended during Operation Desert Storm—a total of 278—are being replaced by Block 3 models. A total production run of 1,085 all-new Block 3 models are expected to be produced from Fiscal Year 1994 through Fiscal Year 1998, at an estimated cost of about $1.4 billion. In addition, all existing Block 2 C-variant and D-variant Tomahawks—as many as 1,795—will be retrofitted with the Block 3 upgrades when they come in for periodic overhaul.

The Block 3 upgrades do not represent the last word in improvements. A constant effort is maintained to develop technologies that might find their way onto the Tomahawk in the years ahead. For example, as these words are written, an initiative is under way to develop a new software package that will minimize the risk of collateral damage during land-attack Tomahawk strikes. This is seen as a necessary safeguard against missiles landing off-target and causing death and destruction in adjacent areas: a residential area, for example, or a school or hospital complex. The new software will assess the missile's performance in flight, and will command it to divert to a predesignated disposal area if its accuracy falls below a preset standard. The disposal area might be an uninhabited region of desert, or a little-used stretch of river. Its precise location, and the abort criteria, will be defined prior to launch by mission planners.

In cases where the missile's accuracy is below standard, but only slightly, the new software will command it to fly to an alternative target where collateral damage would be less consequential. Again, the location of the secondary target, and the criteria for rerouting, will be defined prior to launch by mission planners. The new software also facilitates a higher degree of BIT (built-in self-test) capability than conventionally-armed Tomahawks have had hitherto. BIT both assesses the missile's general airworthiness and verifies the health of its systems prior to launch.

When the new software is released to the US Navy fleet in 1995, missiles receiving it will be known as Precision Strike Tomahawks (PSTs). Although development of the PST capability was not part of the Block 3 upgrade program, it will replace the software package currently employed by Block 3 missiles.

Another initiative has been the development of a limited shipborne mission planning capability. Hitherto, Tomahawk missions could only be planned at a small number of facilities ashore. Current plans call for a limited shipborne mission planning capability (aboard the US Navy aircraft carrier USS *Nimitz*) to achieve IOC status in March 1995. Before long, mission planners aboard many US Navy ships will be able to modify existing Tomahawk strike plans or formulate entirely new ones as required. The idea of an Afloat Planning System (APS) has been around for the best part of a decade. A prototype shipborne Tomahawk mission planning system was installed aboard the amphibious command vessel USS *Mount Whitney* for exploratory tests in late 1992. Those tests were completed in March 1993. A production-specification version of the APS was then installed aboard the *Mount Whitney*, and was undergoing opera-

tional testing as this book closed for press.

Plans call for the APS to be installed aboard command ships and aircraft carriers, thereby ensuring that it is an integral asset of any task force.

Block 4—and beyond

The next major step in the ongoing effort to improve the Tomahawk is the Block 4 upgrade program, also known as the Tomahawk Baseline Improvement Program (T-BIP), which builds on experience gained during the Gulf War. The Block 4 program is currently entering the engineering and manufacturing development (EMD) phase. When it reaches fruition, it will represent a fundamental shift in the way Tomahawks are employed. The missile has previously been regarded primarily as a strategic weapon for use in the opening stages of a conflict—indeed, that was how it was employed in the Gulf War—but it is set to evolve into a tactical weapon capable of undertaking a wide variety of missions throughout the course of hostilities. The acronym TMMM (for Tomahawk Multi-Mission Missile) is being applied to the Block 4 missile, to reflect the fact that it will be capable of undertaking both antiship and land-attack missions.

Block 4 Tomahawks will carry the new WDU-36B warhead, thereby benefitting (as Block 3 missiles do) from the increase in range bestowed by the additional fuel that can be stored around it. Another warhead, capable of penetrating hardened targets—the Tomahawk Hardened Target Penetrator (THTP)—is also under development. Block 4 missiles will parallel their Block 3 cousins in several other respects: they will have an inertial guidance set (although it will be an improved-specification unit), a radar altimeter, and a GPS receiver. GPS may actually supplant TERCOM completely in the Block 4 missile: a final decision has yet to be made. To further reduce the possibility of jamming by enemy defenses, the Block 4 missile's GPS receiver will be even more comprehensively protected.

The two most significant departures from previous practice will be the incorporation of a forward-looking passive infrared sensor system and the inclusion of a two-way data link to enable friendly forces to communicate with the Tomahawk in flight and the missile to relay data back.

With the forward-looking infrared sensor, the Block 4 Tomahawk will be able to employ two alternative methods of terminal navigation, depending on the nature of the target. In one mode it will use its passive infrared sensor to acquire the target, then home in on it—continuously revising its estimate of the aim point, as the B-variant, antiship Tomahawk does. Employing the homing mode, the Pentagon expects to improve the accuracy of Tomahawk strikes by at least 50 percent. In the other mode, once the missile has reached the target area, it will briefly pop up to a higher altitude, employ its infrared sensor in a manner akin to the DSMAC system to image reference objects situated near to the target, compare the scan with a stored wireframe image (a variation on the offset navigation method), then dive down to strike it.

A forward-looking infrared sensor system was selected in favor of rival technologies, such as millimeter-wave radar and lidar (laser imaging detection and ranging), because it has reached a higher state of maturity.

With the two-way data link, Block 4 Tomahawks will be able to relay real-time images to human controllers. For example, a Tomahawk could transmit a short burst of imagery immediately prior to impact, confirming whether the target

was struck. Although this would be a rudimentary method of damage assessment by comparison to undertaking detailed analysis of imagery supplied by reconnaissance satellites or aircraft, it offers the benefit of being instantaneous, allowing mission planners to reduce the number of missiles expended on specific strikes (from 30 to 18, according to an uncorroborated account of a simulation of one particular strike).

A two-way data link would also allow human controllers to locate targets of opportunity and steer the missile into them, or to aim the missile at a specific point on a target: for example, one end of a building as opposed to the other. The video link would only be activated once the Tomahawk is in the general area of the target, to reduce the chance of enemy detection and/or jamming.

Mission controllers could use the two-way data link to retarget a Tomahawk in flight, if necessary. For example, if an earlier strike had not had the desired effect, a missile heading for a less important target could be rerouted to finish the job. Due to the fact that the range of the data link—on the order of several hundred miles—is considerably less than the range of the missile, a manned aircraft (fixed- or rotary-wing), an unmanned aerial vehicle (UAV), or a communications satellite, would have to serve as a relay between the human controller and the Tomahawk. One scenario under consideration has the human controller aboard a supporting manned aircraft flying a safe distance away from the target area.

In the past, it was considered unwise to equip the Tomahawk with a means of emitting signals, because it increased the risk of enemy detection. That view has changed since the ending of the Cold War—or, rather, the circumstances have changed. With the likelihood of a threat from the nations that made up the former Soviet Union diminishing, the possibility of regional conflicts has grown, promoting a reexamination of the benefits data links can offer. It was concluded that the tactical benefits far exceeded the potential drawbacks. Of course, mission planners have the option of not employing the data link on a given strike, or of only using it in brief bursts.

With this departure from the operating philosophy that has characterized the Tomahawk since its conception, the Block 4-specification missile will have much in common with the US Navy's Standoff Land Attack Missile (SLAM) although that has a much shorter range than the Tomahawk. SLAM is essentially a Harpoon antiship missile equipped with an infrared seeker of the type fitted to the Maverick air-to-surface missile, plus a two-way data link (the same one fitted to the Walleye guided bomb), and a GPS receiver.

McDonnell Douglas Aerospace-East and Hughes Missile Systems Company were competing for the Block 4 development contract as this book went to press. A decision as to which contender will be awarded the contract was scheduled for mid-summer 1994. The first

batch of Block 4 Tomahawks will likely be created by converting the remaining B-variant, antiship missiles.

Beyond Block 4, 'stealth' technologies will doubtless be employed to help the Tomahawk, or its replacement, evade enemy detection. The USAF's AGM-129 Advanced Cruise Missile (ACM), stealthy successor to the AGM-86 ALCM, exemplifies this approach. Its fuselage has a flattened underside, which contributes to lift, into which a flush-mounted engine air inlet is set, reducing the missile's radar signature. The engine exhaust is located under the tail, to mask the flow of hot gases from the infrared sensors of enemy aircraft or satellites positioned overhead.

Looking further into the future, cruise missiles may well prove to be the best means of delivering a variety of new, *non-lethal* chemical and biological agents that could revolutionize the present approach to limited-scale warfare. One chemical agent under development destroys aircraft tires when sprayed onto enemy runways and taxiways, while a biological agent containing certain microbes, when introduced into jet fuel storage tanks, turns their contents to jelly. A better way to wage war?

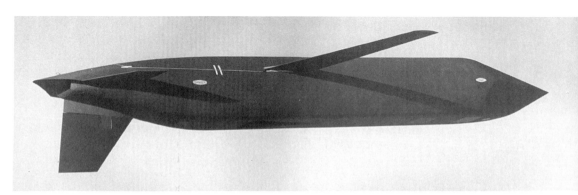

Very much in evidence on the USAF's AGM-129 Advanced Cruise Missile (ACM) are the   *'stealth' technologies that will help future cruise missiles evade enemy detection.*

Index